AS in a W...

Sociology

...Orr-Love,
Abbey College, Birmingham
Series Editor: Kevin Byrne

WPk

Where to find the information you need

SUCCESS OR YOUR MONEY BACK

Letts' market leading series AS in a Week gives you everything you need for exam success. We're so confident that they're the best revision books you can buy that if you don't make the grade we will give you your money back!

HERE'S HOW IT WORKS

Register the Letts AS in a Week guide you buy by writing to us within 28 days of purchase with the following information:

- Name
- Address
- Postcode
- Subject of AS in a Week book bought

Please include your till receipt

To make a **claim**, compare your results to the grades below. If any of your grades qualify for a refund, make a claim by writing to us within 28 days of getting your results, enclosing a copy of your original exam slip. If you do not register, you won't be able to make a claim after you receive your results.

CLAIM IF...

You are an AS (Advanced Subsidiary) student and do not get grade E or above.

You are a Scottish Higher level student and do not get a grade C or above.

This offer is not open to Scottish students taking SCE Higher Grade, or Intermediate qualifications.

Letts Educational
Chiswick Centre
414 Chiswick High Road
London W4 5TF
Tel: 020 8996 3333
Fax: 020 8742 8390
e-mail: mail@lettsed.co.uk
website: www.letts-education.com

Registration and claim address:
Letts Success or Your Money Back Offer, Letts Educational, 414 Chiswick High Road, London, W4 5TF

TERMS AND CONDITIONS

1. Applies to the Letts AS in a Week series only
2. Registration of purchases must be received by Letts Educational within 28 days of the purchase date
3. Registration must be accompanied by a valid till receipt
4. All money back claims must be received by Letts Educational within 28 days of receiving exam results
5. All claims must be accompanied by a letter stating the claim and a copy of the relevant exam results slip
6. Claims will be invalid if they do not match with the original registered subjects
7. Letts Educational reserves the right to seek confirmation of the level of entry of the claimant
8. Responsibility cannot be accepted for lost, delayed or damaged applications, or applications received outside of the stated registration/claim timescales
9. Proof of posting will not be accepted as proof of delivery
10. Offer only available to AS students studying within the UK
11. SUCCESS OR YOUR MONEY BACK is promoted by Letts Educational, 414 Chiswick High Road, London, W4 5TF
12. Registration indicates a complete acceptance of these rules
13. Illegible entries will be disqualified
14. In all matters, the decision of Letts Educational will be final and no correspondence will be entered into

Every effort has been made to trace copyright holders and obtain their permission for the use of copyright material. The authors and publishers will gladly receive information enabling them to rectify any error or omission in subsequent editions.

First published 2000
Reprinted 2002

Text © Michael Orr-Love 2000
Design and illustration © Letts Educational Ltd 2000

British Library Cataloguing in Publication Data
A CIP record for this book is available from the British Library.

ISBN 1 84085 366 2

Prepared by *specialist* publishing services, Milton Keynes

Printed in the UK

Letts Educational Limited is a division of Granada Learning Limited, part of the Granada Media Group

Theories and Methods

5 minutes

Test your knowledge

1 Functionalism likens society to a _____, which stresses the importance of the interdependence of different institutions.

2 Marxists argue that society is based on _____ between two distinct social groups: the _____ and the _____ .

3 Social action theory focuses on how individuals derive _____ from different events.

4 _____ _____ looks at the interaction between individuals. _____ stresses that there is no such thing as true 'objective' facts. _____ seeks to uncover and explain how people make sense of different social settings.

5 The natural sciences provide _____ data. Sociology that attempts to emulate the scientific approach is known as _____ .

6 _____ research produces numerical data. _____ research relies on observation.

7 Popper particularly criticises _____ because its predictions cannot be _____. In Kuhn's analysis of science, he describes _____ , which structure the ways of observing natural phenomena. The 'realists' argue that, like sociology, the sciences often deal with _____ systems.

✔ **If you got them all right, skip to page 10**

3

25 minutes

Improve your knowledge

Sociological Theory

1 The **functionalist** account seeks to explain the normal (and abnormal) functioning of society, which involves studying its different parts to establish objective 'social facts'. This perspective contends that society is made up of various institutions, the most basic being the family. Institutions can be defined as groups of people organised for specific purposes, which interact together. These institutions belong to four **sub-systems**: **economic** (e.g. factories), **political** (e.g. political parties), **kinship** (families) and **cultural** (e.g. schools). The **collective conscience** consists of the values that everybody shares (supported by reactions to crime and religious ceremonies). Society is likened to a biological organism – as the **body** is reliant on *all* organs working properly, so is society. Social institutions are interdependent on one another, as are people. People are born with different abilities and only a few can hold important positions and take decisions. Functionalists stress the importance of society recognising and utilising the whole range of talent and people are rewarded according to their importance and specialist contribution to society (hence doctors are paid more than road sweepers). However, this only works because society is based on a moral consensus. These social values are learnt through different people and institutions (for example, the school and family). **Functionalism** also stresses that change occurs when it has to. For example, education expanded because of the need for a more literate and educated workforce. A central theme of functionalism is that the individual is formed by society.

2 Central to the **Marxist** analysis is to account for class **conflict** rather than **consensus**. Marxism states that conflict occurs because society is constructed upon an economic base (capitalism), which determines social relations. This conflict is between the most powerful, who own the means of production (**bourgeoisie** or ruling class) and the working class (**proletariat**) who sell their labour. **Marx** argued that conflict arises because each class will pursue its own interests. However, the ruling group owns the means to protect its interests and passes on its ideology as 'common-sense' and natural. The media, religion, education, etc. are 'tools' that mask the exploitative nature of capitalism. For example, education ensures that working-class children fail and they accept this as just and natural (**false consciousness**). Inequalities in wealth are not necessary or inevitable.

Using the work of Hegel, Marx argued that history can be divided into epochs, and a certain type of conflict distinguishes each one (this is known as dialectical materialism). Eventually, conflict becomes so large and so far undermines the power base that it is challenged and replaced by a new set of social relations (new order). This forms the basis of Marx's 'science', leading him to predict that capitalism (like all other historical periods) would collapse under the weight of its own contradictions and that the proletariat would assume (communal) control.

The **structural** accounts (namely, Marxism and functionalism) described above can be subjected to a number of criticisms. For example, Marxism is seen as too economically deterministic, reducing or explaining all social phenomenons according to economic relations, when the behaviour of individuals is often more complex. Likewise, functionalism is criticised for placing too much power in the structure of society rather than acknowledging that people are free-thinking beings. It also emphasises solidarity and harmony because many institutions are often dysfunctional. On the other hand, the Marxist division of society into two distinct classes (with a couple of variations) is too simplistic.

3 **Social action theory** is based on the premise that individuals imprint their own **meaning** on life through social interaction rather than being directed by and reacting to larger external forces. **Weber** was interested in unearthing the meaning people attached to a particular event/action. This is not to say that social action theory disregards the influence of institutions. It acknowledges a two-way process: that individuals create and interact with institutions (for example, the organisation of the NHS) which have a bearing on people's lives. Instead of finding definitive 'social facts', social action theory looks for causal explanations, which motivate action.

4 **Interpretative** perspectives, in contrast to the **structural** or **macro** accounts above, look instead at the smaller (**micro**) picture. **Symbolic interactionism**, primarily associated with **George Mead**, stresses that society is created through people's communication and interaction with one another. Individuals use language to negotiate social roles and become aware of themselves through the reactions of others. In different social contexts, people will behave, communicate and see themselves differently. This approach is less formulaic than functionalist and Marxist accounts because it also allows a deeper understanding of how individuals actually interact with one another and institutions. **Phenomenology** is a philosophical rather than sociological position that stresses that there is no such thing as 'true' objective facts or knowledge. It is argued that shared experiences and knowledge amongst people creates the impression of a social order. **Ethnomethodology** ignores the notion that there is a social order, arguing instead that people make their own sense of order. It contends that the external social order described by other sociologists is a false categorisation and imposition. It seeks to uncover how people make sense in different social settings.

Feminism in its various guises is concerned with patriarchal (male) power and domination. **Liberal feminism** focuses on socialisation and sex-role conditioning, whereas **Marxist feminism** looks at women's oppression within the nature of capitalist society. **Radical feminism** is a distinct body of work, which locates men as central to the oppression of women.

Structuralism (**Levi-Strauss**) is a theory of language and culture which constrains free-will/thinking, whereas **post-structuralism** (**Michel Foucault**) argues that language reflects power – language directs us to think about things in a certain way. These are known as discourses, which are socially and historically specific.

Giddens' 'Structuration' is a theoretical/practical position which links the **structural** and the **phenomenological** approaches in sociology. He suggests that there are rules structuring life which people must follow. However, people will react and interact differently with them.

Methodology

5 The methods used by **natural science** are often held as a template of good practice because they provide **verifiable** information (i.e. information which can be checked and proven). Scientists usually work with a **hypothesis** by conducting experiments and observing the outcomes. This often takes place in laboratories, where conditions can be controlled. This relies on the systematic collection of data, which is then tested against the hypothesis. If the hypothesis is correct, then it becomes a law (or 'fact').

Because 'natural' laws have been discovered, the aim of the sociologists (particularly **Auguste Comte**, who described sociology as **social physics**), was to find the 'laws' of society. This approach is known as **positivism** – there are social facts out there ready to be found. However, few sociologists since have shared Comte's enthusiasm for applying the methods of natural science to sociology.

First, there are **ethical reasons**, which prevent humans being 'experimented' on. Second, humans will not behave in the same way in a laboratory as elsewhere because it is a false environment. Instead, **Durkheim** introduced the concept of the **comparative historical method** as an alternative to the laboratory experiment. He believed that if he applied a systematic comparison of similar phenomenon in different contexts (as he did in his **suicide** study) patterns or **correlations** could be established.

6 **Primary sociological research** can essentially take two forms:

- quantitative
- qualitative.

Quantitative research produces **numerical data**, which involves the use of questionnaires (social surveys) and structured interviews. The attempt is to be **objective** (scientific) by locating and explaining social 'facts'. It is obvious that not all of society can be interviewed so **samples** need to be accurate to make surveys as representational as possible.

Qualitative research relies on **observation** (participant and non-participant) and unstructured interviews, which produce descriptive accounts of the participants' lives and actions (Willis, *Learning to Labour*). This approach is **anti-positivist** because it rejects the methods above. However, it is worth noting that many sociologists and researchers often do *not* set themselves strict boundaries to work within. They often use a combination of different methods, which is known as **triangulation**. More often than not, the researcher will choose the methodology which best serves the focus of the study (for example, voting patterns will be best explained numerically).

Sociologists also make use of **secondary sources**; for example **official statistics**, **historical sources** (for comparison), **personal documents** (diaries and letters) and the mass **media**.

7 One of the most debated areas of sociology is the notion that sociology is a science. If the accepted definition of science is one which is based on the testing of a hypothesis by positivistic methodology, then sociology cannot be a science because it rarely produces results that are as precise and repeatable as those produced by natural sciences. People are also very different subjects to plants or simple organisms – they do not just react, they make sense of what happens to them. We can say that people are predictably unpredictable!

Popper argues that sociology cannot be scientific and is extremely critical of **Marxism** in particular. Popper argues that Marxism is unscientific because it is based on ideology and prophecy, which are essentially unscientific. This is because Marx's work cannot be tested. Central to Popper's argument is that Marx's predictions cannot be **falsified** because they have never taken place.

Thomas Kuhn argues that science is not a '**monument of objectivity**' and that it is **revered** too much. It does not actually operate in the objective way that Popper claims. Scientists work within a **paradigm** and this influences the direction of their work. Scientists tend to look for data that refines or adds to that paradigm. Other data that does not fit into the accepted paradigm is rejected as 'noise'. Kuhn contends that there may be other reasons for sustaining the paradigm (for example, maintaining academic or scientific reputations). However, when the paradigm is confronted with too many contradictions it is rejected and replaced by another. What may be irrefutably true today will probably be replaced by another 'truth' in the future. Again, this point of view argues that sociology cannot be scientific because it does not have one all-embracing paradigm but many competing ones, which are unlikely to converge.

Keat, Urry and Sayer (cited in **Haralambos and Holborn** 1998), in their analysis of **'open'** and **'closed'** systems, show that sociology is primarily concerned with open systems, where variables cannot be controlled. Despite Popper's assertion that science works within what Keat, Urry and Sayer describe as a closed system (the **variables are controlled and measured**), the natural sciences often work in open systems as well and precise predictions cannot be made. For example, doctors are practitioners of science but they cannot predict with complete certainty. From this point of view, a great deal of sociology can be considered as scientific because, like the natural sciences, it attempts to provide objective explanations of complex situations.

30 minutes

Use your knowledge

1 Is sociology a science?

2 Account for the differences between structural and social action theories.

5
minutes

Test your knowledge

1. Sociologists describe the non-biological process of human development as _____.

2. Functionalist theory describes two forms of socialisation: _____ socialisation takes place in the home, whereas _____ socialisation takes place at _____ .

3. Marxists argue that rules and regulations are necessary. However, they suggest that people are socialised into a _____ _____ .

4. _____ _____ concentrate on how people make sense of the world through everyday interaction and communication.

5. _____ and _____ believe that the behaviour and characteristics of men and women are genetically pre-programmed. On the other hand, feminists have shown that gendered roles are not natural, but _____ _____.

6. Early theorists have suggested that humans can be divided into types/sub-species. However, sociologists prefer to describe ethnicity as a _____ _____ .

7. Anderson describes national identity as an '_____ _____' which binds anonymous people together.

8. For Bourdieu, social class offers a _____ that charts realistic possibilities and targets.

9. Research on youth tends to concentrate on _____ ___-_____ groups.

10. The 'picking and mixing' of different identities characterises the ___-_____ condition.

Answers

1 culture 2 primary, secondary, school 3 false consciousness 4 Symbolic interactionists 5 Tiger, Fox, social constructs 6 social construct 7 imagined community 8 trajectory 9 deviant sub-cultural 10 post-modern

 If you got them all right, skip to page 22

25 minutes

Improve your knowledge

1 Socialisation

Despite Margaret Thatcher's assertion that there is no such thing as society, but only individuals and families, we can safely assume (to borrow and bend a famous term) that no person or family is an island. All but a few people are products of the interaction they have with society, and sociology seeks to explain those processes. In general, most sociologists would describe these non-biological processes of development (as opposed to other species' instincts) as **cultural**. Essentially, humans become human because they have a complex set of 'needs' (beyond pure survival – shelter, food, procreation) which are realised through the social/cultural interaction they have with other humans. The process that humans are exposed to from birth is known as **socialisation**.

2 Functionalism

It is through socialisation that humans learn the skills for life (known as **norms and values**). This is an active process whereby the child negotiates its way through the complex web of early life. By doing so it learns norms – types of acceptable behaviour which are learnt and expressed in a **social context**. The **functionalist** explanation of socialisation stresses the importance each institution (for example, the family or school) has in shaping society's norms and values and instilling them into individuals. According to **Parsons**, the family is responsible for **primary socialisation** where children learn the simple differences of right and wrong and so on. **Secondary socialisation** takes place at **school**, where children move from **particularistic** or **ascribed** values to **universal** ones (applicable to all). It acts as a 'bridge' between the family and the outside world. The rules and regulations that pupils must follow and the necessity for co-operation and competition at the same time prepare the children for the real world. Likewise, other institutions reflect and support the consensus for the maintenance of stable society. The police uphold the law whilst the media report and condemn when rules, values and norms have been breached. They reflect the general will of the population.

3 Marxism

Marxists believe that society needs rules and regulations (**informal**, i.e. cultural and **formal**, i.e. embodied in law), which act as guidelines or constraints on the individual's behaviour. It would seem from the outset that there is an unlikely convergence of opinion between **functionalists** and **Marxists**, who both argue that rules and regulations are necessary and inevitable in the smooth day-to-day running of society. However, Marxists do not celebrate the intricate interrelationship of institutions and values. Instead they describe the disastrous and insidious impact that capitalist society has on individuals by instilling in them a '**false consciousness**' through '**ideological state apparatus**' such as school and the media and '**repressive state institutions**' such as the police and judiciary (**Althusser**). The norms and values of society are in fact **bourgeois** norms and values, which help mask and prop up the exploitative nature of capitalist society. People's 'real' interests, (or, more specifically, the working class's interests) appear to be served by institutions like schools, but these are deceitful measures to train and condition the population into a life of mass compliance – described by **Bowles and Gintis** as the '**hidden curriculum**'. This 'ideological domination', also known as the hegemony, is achieved by offering concessions (e.g. the welfare state). The crux of the argument is that the **superstructure** does not act in the interests of the masses, so individuals are subjected to and are powerless in the face of the capitalist institutional onslaught. Although recent critical thinking has been revised by **Gramsci** and has become more subtle as a consequence, Marxists and neo-Marxists are still interested in explaining why capitalism continues despite its inherent contradictions.

4 'Social Action'

Whilst structuralists look towards society's impact on individuals, Goffman, influenced by the work of Mead and **symbolic interactionism**, favours a position that looks at how social actors negotiate the small, ordinary and trivial aspects that constitute everyday living – the things that are taken for granted. For symbolic interactionists, the continual game of action/reaction by individuals in different social contexts is essential in understanding the process of role playing and socialisation. The 'rules of contact' or social strategies we employ in numerous different social contexts (for example what we should/should not do in a particular time and place) are learnt through the social contact we have with others. Conversations and gestures from others give us our perception of self and thus give structure and meaning to our lives.

Garfinkel (an ethnomethodologist) argues that when the taken-for-granted rules of everyday speech are rebuked, social upset ensues. This is because we learn and therefore take for granted, depending on the context, the implicit meanings of inherently ambiguous terms such as 'Alright?' We learn to answer the question or greeting appropriately and in doing so we have observed a **social ritual** and contributed to the maintenance of normal everyday life without being aware of it. In moments of antagonism we may choose to ignore the social conventions, fully aware that we will cause upset. If this pattern of 'misunderstanding' was repeated on a mass scale one could imagine the consequences it would have for any group that sees itself collectively.

For scholars like Erving Goffman, it is important to distinguish between the private domain (domestic) and public domain (work, shops) in individual behavioural terms because it is the immense pressure of society's norms and values which dictates a person's behaviour in different contexts. So, for example, it is 'normal' for a man to dress as a man and not as a woman. If he chooses to dress as a woman in a public setting (for example, work) there may be consequences or sanctions which may be **formal** (disciplinary action) and/or **informal** (shunned by colleagues) simply because he has failed to observe society's norms. However, in a private setting or different 'public' social setting, his mode of behaviour may be acceptable. The fact that such expressions can often only be made in 'another' setting is testimony to the power of social norms and values.

5 Sex, Sexuality and Gender

However, the notion of value is a problematic one. Foucault's historical analysis of the **discourses** (ways of talking and thinking about a subject) surrounding homosexuality in *The History Of Sexuality* (1977) suggests that homosexuality is incompatible with the reproductive value of the Church's teachings about sex (homosexuality is not procreative). Foucault argues that the puritanical Victorian discourses on sex (which were very similar to those described above) have acted as a 'hangover' on what we hold to be 'normal' today. Indeed, the media 'reflects' or articulates these norms and values. Would the 'outing' of Boyzone's Stephen Gately have been a major tabloid scoop if he had declared that he was heterosexual?

Although there is disagreement amongst scholars about the role of hormones, the physical biological differences between the sexes (male and female) are indisputable. Some scholars argue that gender (masculine and feminine) is a social/cultural role allocation rather than being naturally determined by sex, or being evolutionary or God-given, despite the apparent universality of such differentiation. Others assert that differences in emotions, attitude and roles between the sexes are rooted firmly in the biological, or more specifically, in brain lateralisation (males and females use different parts of the brain) or hormonal differences (testosterone is linked to male aggression, for example).

Other thinkers (**Tiger and Fox**) advocate a teleological (related to purpose rather than cause) reasoning for male/female differences by referring to how humans are pre-programmed to behave a certain way. Male aggression and dominance is contrasted with the 'natural' instinct of female caring and nurturing. Both sexes have genetically inherited and adapted behaviour from their primitive hunting ancestors, which explains why men occupy the most dominant positions, whilst women take on the more subservient and 'natural' role of caring for children. The advantage of keeping such an arrangement is to benefit and continue the genetic patterns of humans (the mother/child bond). Murdock argues that men and women are better suited to certain roles because of biological differences, e.g. men are stronger and are therefore better suited to heavy manual labour. Functionalists have stressed the 'naturalness' of such roles in understanding the make-up of the family and how each gender role functions in a particular way for the good of society as a whole. These distinctions are passed on to offspring and society seems to work best when it is arranged on these lines.

However, our concept of what it is to be a man or a woman, and what is masculine or feminine, is subject to change. This implies a social distinction that dictates and allocates the 'correct' modes of role behaviour in a particular place and time. For example, the traditional view of femininity has been subjected to many challenges at all levels of society, especially in the media. The computer generated heroine of Tomb Raider, Lara Croft, may have a western 'hegemonic sexuality' (slim, athletic body, large breasts) but she challenges the assumption that women are or should be passive and men active.

Feminists have shown how sex role and gender allocation is constant despite taking place in different contexts. Feminists show that the socialisation process is gendered. However, it is the effect of differential socialisation (various studies and anecdotal evidence suggest that it takes place from birth) that can condemn women to a secondary position to men. From the toys that are given to children (boys' toys emphasise leadership and aggression, whereas girls' toys and games emphasise caring and assisting) to the way they are verbally addressed, a social hierarchy develops which positions male activities as being more worthwhile than female. This is reflected and thus extended in school and the world of work, where men usually occupy the more powerful and well-paid occupations.

6 Ethnicity

Sociologists' analysis of ethnicity is analogous of the Marxist view of class relations and can be used, in part, to explain the development of ethnic or minority and conversely national identities. We use the term minority to denote the numerical position of a group in comparison to the ruling majority. Earlier theorists from the 18th and 19th centuries and the writers of some political discourses (especially those who have disseminated racist literature in Nazi Germany) have argued that ethnicity (the term 'race' is often used synonymously) is derived biologically and that humans can be divided into types or different sub-species with different characteristics. This view blurs the cultural and biological (or physical) factors into one. Racial divisions like these are, at best, ethnocentric (or Western-centric) but usually they have taken on a more insidious character, promoting racial superiority of one group over others.

Stereotypes are symptomatic of this process, whereby the characteristics of groups are reduced for the sake of definition, categorisation and differentiation. Characteristics ascribed to groups of people on the basis of race are often perceived as natural and inevitable (for example, that black people have rhythm). Increasingly, the position adopted by most academics is that ethnicity, like gender, is a **social construct**. You may be born into an ethnic identity but you are certainly not born with it. To have an ethnic identity is to acquire a common culture, tradition and set of beliefs with those who may (but may not) have the same 'point of origin'.

7

National identity is a rather nebulous and problematic concept because it is impossible, without gross over-simplification, to pinpoint a nation's core characteristics, especially when one refers to the diaspora of peoples around the world. Many countries are multi-cultural, so ethnicity or the existence of minority groups must by definition challenge the notion of a homogeneous national identity. However, it is these contradictions which are 'masked over' or 'externalised' (**Thompson** 1990) by 'reducing the complexity of the social environment' (**Millar** 1982).

Through numerous different agencies (for example the media), a country constructs a national identity amongst its people by referring to a common past, present and future. A sense of national identity must embrace and bind people who are otherwise 'anonymous strangers' into what **Anderson** calls an **imagined community**. The invention and implementation of new communication networks, especially newspapers, meant that disparate groups of people could form a common consciousness and outlook with others who shared the same (but not immediate) geo-political space. A national identity has to embrace but override local concerns so that all feel united. In Britain, the Union Jack, national anthem, and royal coronations were all 'ideological inventions' (**Gellner**, 1983) of the Victorians intended to forge a link with a shared symbolic past. Furthermore, in school we 'learn' a selective history by celebrating 'great' British culture, personalities and significant events.

Today, the widely celebrated concept of 'Cool Britannia' has given rise to a new or updated version of what it means to be British (young, gifted and rich). These myths perpetuate or reinvent stereotypical ideas of nationhood by conflating the characteristics of all citizens into an all-embracing one (characterised by great individuals). The term 'race' (as discussed earlier) is often used in conjunction with nation, implying that a nation's people have their own distinct characteristics.

Nationality, which is based on ethnicity or a commonality with other people within a given political/geographical territory, is according to **Anderson**, 'the most universally legitimate value in the political life of our time' (1983:12). **Durkheim** argued that as the world became more secular, nationalism would replace religion, and its totems (i.e. flags) would be worshipped instead. In Britain, Scottish, Welsh and Irish national identities are inextricably bound up in their political, cultural, historical and geographic proximity with England, and serve to differentiate these cultures from 'Britishness', which is dominated by 'Englishness'. Sport, according to **Morse** (1983), 'has become one of the most powerful locus of collective identities' and so Scottish football fans, for example, aware of the aggressive stereotypes associated with English football fans, go to great lengths to distance themselves by creating a carnival-like atmosphere at foreign football venues. National identity is not just about how we see ourselves but how we want others to see us.

8 Class

Like gender and ethnicity, class is a division that gives rise to a variety of conflicting tensions. The delineation of people into classes is not as straightforward as the following typology suggests. For example, the numbers employed in manual work and non-manual work have decreased and increased respectively, which suggests that Britain is becoming more middle-class. However the picture is much more complex when we look at the sub-divisions within each strata.

Socialisation, Identity and Youth Culture

The **upper class** can be divided into 'old money' (landed aristocracy) and 'new money' (entrepreneurs). In some cases the distinction is blurred, as the 'new' Victorian upper class used its wealth to buy titles, property and assimilation into the 'old' (Weiner). The **middle class** refers to many occupations and positions held in society. The middle class can be divided into three: the old (small businesspeople such as shopkeepers), the upper (managerial, professional) and lower (teachers, nurses). The **working class** is thought to have two tiers: an upper (skilled manual) and lower (semi- or non-skilled). Some sociologists suggest an **underclass** (the long-term unemployed, those who drift in and out of work and those who experience poor pay and working conditions). Class can be described as an identity that cuts through other cultural distinctions such as gender and ethnicity.

Class and social differentiation for more conservative writers is seen as one of the necessary features of a modern, complex capitalist society. Society requires class, which signifies importance in the social order. For **Marx**, class was central to his critique of capitalism, which described the interests of the bourgeoisie and the proletariat as being diametrically opposed. Capitalism relies on the exploitation and subordination of the working classes by the ruling classes who own the **means of production**. This is achieved not just through stark economic power but, according to **Gramsci and Althusser**, through ideological means as well.

Whilst we can describe class as mass grouping of individuals who have similar occupations and interests, **Bourdieu** took the concept of class further and described the **'habitus'** or the interrelationship and interdependence of material existence (occupation, wealth) and cultural experiences (education, leisure activities) which derived from one's class position. Central to this idea is the concept that class position is not just what occupation somebody holds or how much he or she earns (although this is important to the analysis) but the life choices and values that emanate from holding a particular social position or 'space' in common with others (for example, working as a labourer in heavy industry).

Central to Bourdieu's analysis is **cultural capital**, which is convertible into and reproduced by economical capital (wealth). The economic position of the middle classes, for example, generates a perception and appreciation of life chances (known as **trajectory**). It is this trajectory of realistic possibilities or targets, as **Willis** showed in *Learning To Labour*, which limits or creates opportunities. Whilst the middle classes place huge emphasis on academic work (and deferment of instant gratification) and qualifications, the working class, whose experiences of education are not the same (i.e. are unsuccessful) will 'condemn' themselves to failure by not investing in their future.

Goldthorpe and Lockwood, in their study of Luton car workers, wanted to test the hypothesis that manual workers who were enjoying higher wages were going through an '**embourgeoisement**' process (becoming richer and more privatised). They found that the affluent workers' outlook (which was more hedonistic – more 'here and now' than deferred) and leisure time activities were not the same as those of middle class workers and so remained essentially working class.

Youth Identities

9

The notion of youth, or more specifically the teenager, is a relatively new one. In other words, it is, alongside other identities, socially constructed. On the other hand, certain 'rites of passage', long established in many cultures and societies, are conducted at this adolescent stage to mark the transition into adulthood. Whilst the transition in traditional societies may be a relatively uneventful one (in terms of wider social conflict), the accepted pedagogy in the West (although it is not proven) is that adolescence can be likened to a biological/hormonal volcano ready to erupt – it is a juncture in one's life; a site for recognition and status; a 'natural' battleground to mark the passing from childhood to adulthood.

Earlier writing on youth identities has reflected a preoccupation with conflict and concentrated on the **deviant** (mostly working class) **sub-cultural groups** that have forged opposition or resistance to the dominant values of society (i.e. contempt for authority). Sociological research on youth sub-cultural groups, such as the Teds, Mods and Punks (although class background was less homogeneous in this group) identifies 'style' and music as central components. The ephemeral and recyclable nature of different youth sub-cultures can be understood in a wider social-historical context. The creation of the Teds and Mods sub-cultural groups took place in the relatively prosperous 1950s and 1960s and coincided with the importation of American and European culture and higher incomes for working class youth. Teenagers had independence and leisure opportunities never afforded them before. The hedonism of the 'almost adults' contravened what Cohen describes as the post-war 'boundaries' of acceptability and sobriety and so drew them into conflict with the establishment and older generations.

On the other hand, the Punks forged an (anti-style) identity/expression of 'hegemonic' disenchantment, which **Hebdige** describes as anti-establishment – it attacked what it saw as the disempowering effect of commercialised popular culture (including fashion) and the values and sensibilities of 'normal' people and mainstream society. **Willis** (*Profane Culture,* 1978) describes a similarity to the hippies' challenge and rebuke of 'straight' culture through their 'functionally inappropriate' clothes (1978), unpredictable behaviour, long hair and drug use. By drawing on, comparing and distinguishing the experiences of this typically middle-class 'opt-out' and 'other-worldly' culture with the masculine and tough world of working class biker culture, Willis shows how resistance (in whatever form it takes) cuts through all of society rather than being appropriated just to a disenfranchised and discontented working class youth.

Post-modern Identities

The earlier cultural critics, such as **Leavis** and **Hoggart**, were not convinced that the 'rich', authentic cultural tradition of the working class was replaced by a better form of resistance, describing it as being lost to commercialism and the crude Americanisation of youth culture. Paul Willis' emphasis (*Common Culture: Symbolic Work At Play In The Everyday Cultures Of The Young,* 1990) had much in common with **Williams'** understanding of culture as an active process. However, Willis moves beyond a class-based analysis and argues that youth identity today is characterised less by class but by style, taste and creativity. Most if not all young people work creatively with (i.e. reinterpret) the (homogenised) cultural output of capitalism and this overcomes class differences because the distinctions between high and low culture are blurred. According to Willis, youths no longer identify and empathise with class distinctions because all youth culture is in relation to and is a re-manifestation of the same everyday cultural products. The result is that individuality has flourished. Young people, from whatever class or ethnic background, pick and mix their identities and make sense of their world from a whole range of influences. **McRobbie** gives a celebratory account of **post-modern** youth culture, in which she sees young women breaking free from an all-encompassing gender identity and forging their own, which overrides class identities.

Whilst McRobbie et al point to the empowerment of the young post-modern individual, **Harvey**, in *The Condition of Postmodernity*, concentrates with pessimism on the uncertainty it creates. This is reflected in both the 'commodified' culture and the everyday experiences of individuals. For example, music artists such as Wyclef and Puff Daddy will 'borrow' songs written by other artists and subject them to re-mixing, layering new lyrics. McRobbie identifies an ironic playfulness with the reinterpretation of the text (because it may have emanated from independent individuals) but, like Jameson, Harvey marks this as the 'death of the author', because nothing is really new or original. On the other hand, from an everyday perspective, young people face an altogether less certain future than their predecessors, which is characterised by the increasing fragmentation of collective identities (both national and local) and the loss of fixed career paths (through the de-skilling of some occupations), which are replaced by short-term working contracts.

Post-modernism is characterised by uncertainty and the non-fixture of a common national identity. Different ethnic groups have had an enormous impact on the culture of indigenous communities (for example, one survey found that chicken tikka masala is the most popular English dish). However, the double bind of racism and conflicting or unresolved national identity (pride in ethnic origin) has had a profound impact on the sense of identity of young (mainly working class) Afro-Caribbean and Asian youth. To suggest that their conditions and life experiences are analogous with those of their white counterparts would be a serious oversight. A collective strength based on age, individuality and creativity with commodities does not mask the discrimination and condemnation to an inferior life suffered by many ethnic minorities in the past. Historically, few opportunities in the workplace have been created for ethnic minorities, and this, in part, explains the development of particular deviant sub-cultures in young men. Pryce shows how some young men rejected what appeared to be the continuation of colonialism and adopted resistance by resorting to 'hustling' (illegal ways of making money).

Socialisation, Identity and Youth Culture

30 minutes

Use your knowledge

1 Are social roles natural and inevitable?

2 Compare and contrast structural and interactionist theories of socialisation.

3 How is national identity constructed?

4 Youth culture no longer displays resistance. Discuss.

5 minutes

 Test your knowledge

 1 According to the functionalist Murdock, the _____ family is _____ .

2 Some social commentators have argued that the high incidence of _____ is threatening to the institution of the family.

 3 It is argued that _____ has led to changes in the composition of the family. Today, families are more likely to be _____ and more insular. For Parsons, the modern family is _____ and necessary to modern society.

 4 Murdock identifies four functions in the family. They are _____ , _____ , _____ and _____ . Parsons describes the family as having 'two _____ _____ _____ '. These are _____ socialisation and the _____ of _____ _____ .

5 Engels charts the development of the family alongside the development of _____ _____ . Marxists also contend that the family is responsible for _____ and _____ reproduction, which benefits capitalism.

6 Feminism is concerned with gender _____ and _____ in the family.

 7 The family, according to Leach and Laing, is a divisive, inward-looking institution. They describe this arrangement as a family ' _____ ', where simple divisions of 'them' and 'us' are created and carried through into society.

 **Answers**

1 nuclear, universal 2 divorce 3 industrialisation, smaller, functional 4 sexual, reproductive, economic, socialising, basic irreducible functions, primary, stabilisation (of) adult personalities 5 private property, physical, ideological 6 inequalities, exploitation 7 ghetto

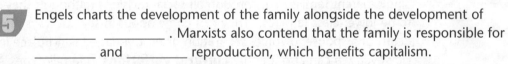 **✔ If you got them all right, skip to page 31**

25 minutes

Improve your knowledge

1 The most common family types (or systems) found in British society are:

- the **nuclear** (or conjugal) family, one in which the parents co-habit with each other and their children;
- the **extended** family, the larger 'network' of relations in the locality (grandparents, uncles, etc.).

The **functionalist**, **Murdock**, described this type of arrangement as **universal**, but two new types of families have emerged. The '**reconstituted**' **family** occurs when children from a previous relationship become part of a new family. This is becoming increasingly common because in Britain one-third of all marriages are re-marriages. Also, more than one million **single-parent families** exist. The proportion of families headed by a lone parent is almost one in four and the lone parent is usually the mother (*Social Trends,* 1997).

Single-parent families cut through all social divisions (although they are more likely to be lower-class families). They can come about in several ways, including the death of a spouse, divorce, separation or no marriage taking place in families. However, we can also identify **cultural variations** in family types. West Indian families tend to be headed by the mother (matriarchal families) and may have no stable father figure present. In the United States, 51% of all black children lived with their mother but not their father (1985). This is set against the importance and emphasis that society places on the nuclear family, which is often taken for granted. Single-parent families are often stigmatised for bearing children who, statistically, are more likely to become involved with criminal activity, claiming benefits and so on. The article 'Abortion cuts crime says study' (the *Guardian,* August 10 1999) reflects this stigmatism. It quotes from the Levitt-Donohue paper which claims that higher abortion rates in the 1970s (which were common in poorer sections of society) led to lower crime rates in the 1980s and 1990s. It concluded that (typically single) women who bear unwanted children are automatically disadvantaged (because poverty often accompanies single-parent families) or neglected (or both), which leads children into social problems and criminal activities later in life.

2 Today, the decline and breakdown of marriages in Britain is held to be the distinguishing feature of changing family structures. Since the 1960s there has been a steady decline in the number of people marrying, whilst cohabitation has increased. Evidence suggests that most couples are increasingly likely to live together before marriage. The stigma attached to births outside marriage has declined and around one in three births are outside wedlock. But rather than being a threat to the family, it might be regarded as a slight variation on an old theme. Many children are born to permanent, marriage-like relationships.

There are increasing numbers of marital breakdowns in Britain. When we refer to marital breakdown, we refer to **divorce** (legal termination) and **formal separation** (when the spouses no longer live in the same dwellings). Another type of breakdown is one that can be described as an **empty shell marriage**, where married couples live together but their marriage exists in name only. Changes in divorce laws have been followed by increases in the divorce rate. These increases may be a reflection of the liberalisation of law, but they may also be a real indication of the number of unhappy marriages (especially for women, because they initiate over 70% of divorces).

It is worth investigating what actually causes divorce. Some commentators have suggested that the increasing economic independence of women makes them less reliant on men. Also, traditional roles are being scrutinised. Increasingly, there is the belief that if women are expected to share the economic burden, then men must contribute to the domestic burden as well. As **Oakley** points out, there is little evidence that husbands share housework. Pressure is heaped upon women if they are still expected to assume primary responsibility for home and family.

Goode points out that, historically, marriages were not based on love but were made for economic reasons. Capitalism has created individuality, and contemporary marriage is based on the premise of love and romance. It is also expected to fulfill an emotional need that society cannot provide. If these conditions are not met then marriages break down. Recently, a radio station offered two complete strangers prizes if they would marry each other before meeting. This attracted a great deal of criticism, especially from the Christian Church, because it had been arranged on the basis of material gain. However, the riposte from one presenter was that it was not the first marriage, nor would it be the last, to be arranged in Birmingham.

Divorce rates are higher amongst working-class and lower middle-class people. This could be a consequence of the economic and social pressure that these couples endure. In addition, couples from different class backgrounds and younger brides and grooms are more likely to divorce. However, it may be premature to ring the death knell for the institution of marriage. It could be argued that marriage as an institution is not weakening, because most people marry at some time (although usually later). The difference is that today they may reject partners.

It is also worth noting that there are other exceptions to the universal nuclear family. The customs of the **Nayar** people of Kerala, Southern India are a cultural example of a non-nuclear family because the cultural environment dictated its form. Women were 'allowed' to be promiscuous so paternity was uncertain. The Nayar were war-like and typically men were absent for long periods of time or killed. Other arrangements were made so that children were produced and reared without the aid of the nuclear family. Instead, brothers assumed responsibility for the protection of the children.

The **Kibbutzim** in Israel and the '**Russian experiment**' are both examples of deliberate attempts to produce collectively based families. The role of the Kibbutzim was to replace and/or supplement the role of family – children were brought up and socialised to the collective values of the community rather than individuality. Today, however, its role has been diluted somewhat. Children often sleep at their family home rather than just have a few hours contact each day as previously advocated. The 'Russian experiment' was both an ideological and practical construction to undermine the institution of the family (see Marx and Engel's arguments below) and release women from the home so they could assist in Russia's reconstruction. Wide-scale crèche and nursery facilities were provided.

 There is very little consensus amongst sociologists on how the family has been affected by **industrialisation** and modernisation. This section will look at the competing explanations for the different **developmental stages** of family composition.

The common starting point is to describe the pre-industrial family. This is described as characteristic of **non-literate societies**, where the family is the central organising principle of life; a unit of production who work as a team (hence surnames based on occupation – Baker, Smith, etc.). Such a family is also known as the '**classic' extended family**, which was headed by the father, who directed the activities of the rest of the family. **Laslett** argues that the 'classic' extended family was not as prevalent as originally thought. **Anderson**, using data from the 1851 Census, argues that the pre-industrial period was characterised by a huge diversity of family types – no one type predominated. For example, in industrial times, a number of families (23%) could be described as extended. These tended to emerge during times of hardship, offering mutual aid.

According to **Willmott and Young**, the 'stage two' or **early industrial family** was typically extended. Like Anderson they contend that family networks extended during times of difficulty. During this period families came together in response to low wages. Women also set up informal networks of support to assist one another. Mortality rates for men, due to wars and industrial accidents, were much higher than they are today, so many women became heads of households. These patterns continued well into the 1950s (**Bethnal Green study**). However, it is widely believed that the emergence of industrialisation, with high rates of geographical and social mobility, weakened kinship ties and dependency on the extended family.

Parsons argues that the typical modern or 'stage three' family is the 'isolated nuclear family' which exists in 'structural isolation'. Parsons argues that there is a reduced need for kinship groups because many institutions have taken over the functions once performed by families (for example, schools, business firms and hospitals). Wilmott and Young describe the modern family as the **symmetrical family**, in which spouses are home-centred (having access to more amenities); they share work, decisions and so on. More recent sociological research has suggested that 'extended family' ties are still maintained but in different ways. For example, family members do not feel obliged but choose to remain in contact with other kin. Very few people actually sever all ties with close relations.

Parsons argues that the modern family is necessary and **functional** because it meets the requirements of the economic system (a small mobile isolated unit is ideal). Parsons argues that changing values complement the shift from one family type to another. The traditional/extended family **ascribed status** to members according to their role in the family (usually older males would head the hierarchy), whereas modern industrial society has universal values where status is achieved outside the family. **Achieved status** would be potentially damaging to larger families whose hierarchies are structured on a dated criteria. If the offspring achieve a higher status than the head of the family, it undermines the head's authority. According to Parsons, the same situation cannot arise in the nuclear family because there is not a conflict of values. However, students should take care not to assume that modern families are harmonious. Because social/gender roles have been traditionally delineated, tensions often arise when women become the chief wage earner.

Harris takes issue with the premise of Parsons' work. In opposition, Harris suggests that the structure and organisation of families actually contributed to the beginning of industrialisation rather than industrialisation creating the families we know today. Primogeniture (inheritance) created the 'ideal' family for industrialisation. Because ownership was passed on to the eldest, those who did not inherit had to move and search for employment elsewhere.

Today, families are predominantly nuclear rather than extended. They are also **smaller**. Since 1971, most households contain only one or two people. But the family unit, despite the changing economic and social environment, remains strong.

 The **functionalist** account articulated primarily by Murdock and Parsons maintains that the nuclear family is the best **organisational basis** for society.

Murdock identifies four functions of the family. The first two, **sexual** and **reproductive**, provide and contain the sex drive whilst ensuring that paternity is certain. It is his assertion that the family (two parents) is the best and most efficient way to bring up children. He refers to a gender-based division of labour (man as breadwinner and woman as homemaker). As a unit, it also has an important **economic** function, by providing food and shelter. **Bell and Vogel** expand Murdock's third point, arguing that the family contributes best to and benefits from the other sub-systems (for example, the economy provides goods and services, the family purchases them). Finally, the family is responsible for the **socialisation** of children. Without this there would be no culture and thus no society.

Parsons insists that the family has two '**basic irreducible functions**'. They are **primary socialisation** and the **stabilisation of adult personalities**. Primary socialisation is the teaching of shared norms and values – it assimilates the young individual into the dominant culture. Secondly, the stabilisation of the adult personality is achieved because the family acts as an escape from the trials and tribulations of everyday life. It acts as a sanctuary by helping people to let off steam or calm themselves before they re-enter the outside world.

 The **Marxist** perspective asserts that:

- the nuclear family is not universal but a **product of capitalism**;
- the family is an **exploitative institution**.

Engels' work offers a historical perspective on gender relations and male dominance. He refutes the biological justification for the gender-based division of labour. He describes the earlier stages of human evolution as having a degree of sex-equality (characterised by promiscuity), where the means of production were communally owned. As roles became more individualised and specialised and dominated by men (which produced a 'need' for the exchange of one's own labour with another), the monogamous nuclear family evolved, which restricted the sexual liberty of individuals (to ensure paternity was known). This type of family appeared with the emergence of **private property**. As men had gained control of wealth, they passed it on to their male offspring (primogeniture), and this acted as justification for and legitimised male domination of the family.

Although the patriarchal nuclear family predates capitalism, Marx argued that it fitted in within the demands of capitalism. Central to Marxist discourse is the notion of exploitation – the family is a continuation of the exploitative set of relations described above. It has also been seen in terms of sexual possessiveness of marital partners. **Marx** argued that marriage '**is incontestably a form of exclusive private property**', where the woman gives sex in return for economic security (Engels described this as '**glorified prostitution**'). The female partner, by being put in this position, is exploited by the male partner.

It is also argued that families ensure the continuation of capitalism through **ideological and physical reproduction**. The family is merely a 'tool' for moulding a future workforce by passing on those values (passivity, hard work, discipline, and respect for authority) which support the structures of capitalism (Feeley). Furthermore, the next generation of workers are brought up at no extra cost to the system.

6 This section looks at **feminist** discussions on the role of the family. It is suggested that:

- women experience genuine **inequalities** in society and this is reflected in family relations;
- there is a dark side to family life.

The **Marxist feminist** position is one that focuses on the '**double' exploitation** of women by capitalism and men. The family also acts as strong discipline to commit people to wage labour. It can also act as a safety valve so that the system is not threatened by frustration and pressures of work. This position focuses on how this safety valve actually works. In many cases it can be the partner (usually the woman) who acts not only as an emotional sounding board but also as a physical punch bag. The separation of 'them' and 'us' makes families inherently anti-social (**Barrett and McIntosh**) by devaluing other ways of life. At the same time it is an effective way of hiding physical and mental abuse.

The radical feminist approach describes the oppression of women as the most fundamental form of domination. **Delphy and Leonard** describe the family as an economic system in which men rather than capitalism benefit from the exploitation of women's labour. **Oakley** adds to this, arguing that the family does not benefit women. In return, women receive dull work, little or no pay and low status. In addition to the economic responsibilities, women often find themselves in the role of 'husband supporter', offering sex, relaxation, support etc. For example, women are more likely to suppress their own feelings so they can provide emotional care. There are two sinister outcomes to this arrangement. Women in marriages are more likely to suffer from mental illness or be subjected to abuse by partners who vent their anger at them. This is far from the almost perfect situation described by the functionalists.

Other feminist accounts focus on how discourses position women as 'motherly', 'domestic', 'caring', etc. From birth, males and females are subjected to gendered socialisation, which stresses the naturalism of gender roles – this ultimately leads to the exploitation of females. Because women are oppressed in the public sphere, (**Brownmiller** argues that women are controlled through the fear of attack and rape) they are led to believe that the private sphere is where women are safe to fully express themselves.

7 **Leach** and **Laing** argue that the isolation of modern nuclear families has a dysfunctional effect on society. Leach claims that the family becomes overloaded by the demands placed on it and this results in conflict. Furthermore, families become insular and suspicious of outsiders. The modern family breeds fear of the outside world and creates barriers. Laing's analysis describes the family as an unhealthy and uncertain arrangement where divisions and alliances are made between different members of the family creating a Mafiosi-type situation. Laing's '**family ghetto**' converges with Leach's notion that the problems of the family can create problems in society. Simple divisions of 'them' and 'us' are created within the family and children learn to apply these distinctions to wider society (e.g. black/white).

Sociology of the Family and Households

30 minutes

Use your knowledge

1. The nuclear family is universal. Discuss.

2. How has the composition of families changed over the last three centuries?

3. Is the family the best organisational basis for society?

5 minutes

Test your knowledge

 Functionalists argue that religion helps to sustain _____ _____ in times of transition and stress.

 Karl Marx described religious ideas as _____ ideas. He also argued that religion dulls the pain of _____ by promising eternal bliss in the afterlife.

 Central to Weber's analysis was that religion could cause change rather than maintain the social order. _____ was particularly influential in the development of capitalism.

 Troeltsch describes three types of religious organisations: _____ tend to be large religious organisations which are close to the state, _____ are described as 'watered down', whereas _____ are much smaller and more integrated.

 The _____ debate is one which focuses on the decline of religion in modern society. However, it is argued that, through _____ , newly introduced religions such as _____ have re-opened the debate on religion in Britain.

 Answers

1 social solidarity 2 human, oppression 3 Calvinism, 4 churches, denominations, sects 5 secularisation, immigration, Islam

✔ **If you got them all right, skip to page 38**

25 minutes

Improve your knowledge

1 The **functionalist** account of religion explains:

- how religion acts as a collective expression of society
- how religion helps to sustain **social solidarity** in times of transition and stress.

Functionalism stresses that social life is impossible without shared values and moral beliefs. Their absence equals no social order and no society. Religion therefore reinforces the collective conscience. It strengthens the values and moral beliefs that form the basis of society. By coming together, people recognise the importance of the social group and their dependence upon it – unity is strengthened through collective worship and religious rituals. **Durkheim** (*The Elementary Forms of Religious Life*, 1912) argued that to understand the role of religion in society we have to understand the relationship between the sacred and the profane (non-religious). Each religion has symbols or 'totems', which stand for the values central to the community. Religion offers a focus; the religious congregation is a social congregation, which brings people together and binds them in a shared experience. When people worship God, they worship society. Therefore, the religious act is symbolic because humans find it easier to locate and express their feelings towards a sacred object than towards something as complex as society.

Talcott Parsons argued that religion provides for the **cultural** (profane) **system** a framework for human action and standards against which people's conduct can be evaluated. The norms of the social system can be integrated by religious instructions which provide general principles and moral beliefs. **Parsons** also contended that religion's function was to act as a 'release valve' and 'comforter' to people when events seemed to be out of human control. It offers explanations and resolutions to the 'big' questions of life (e.g. 'Why am I here?'), which could be socially destructive.

Malinowski's study of the **Trobriand Islanders** (New Guinea) found, like Durkheim and Parsons, that religion reinforces social norms and values. Malinowski linked religion's importance with situations of anxiety, tension and emotional stress, which threaten or change the order of social solidarity. Moreover, the rituals which accompany such events act as a comforter (funerals express a belief in immortality) and the gathering of the community acts as a gesture of social solidarity and support (celebrating the union of the newlyweds).

Marxist sociologists concentrate on how religion reinforces the status quo. As in functionalism, religion is seen to act as a social 'gel', but Marxists take a less celebratory view, arguing that it 'papers over the cracks' by:

- justifying the social order;
- acting as an anaesthetic.

Marx argued that religious ideas are **human** ideas but are mistakenly identified as God's. God is a human creation, and once humans realise that these ideas do not come from a greater distinct (alien) being, they can take control of their destiny. Humans can do this by utilising the 'good' ideas of religion (treating all humans fairly) to create a utopia (heaven on earth) rather than deferring happiness and fulfilment to the afterlife (which doesn't exist anyway). Religion is an illusion that justifies and legitimises the subordination of the working classes and the domination and the privilege of the dominant class. Historically, the ruling classes have used religion to justify their position both to themselves and to others (for example, the concept of the divine right of kings and queens). Religion is an **ideology** – a system of thoughts and ideas – which constitutes the deceptive ruling class orthodoxy. Marx wrote:

> *'Religion is the sigh of the oppressed creature, the sentiment of a heartless world and the soul of soulless conditions. It is the opium of the people.'*

It dulls the pain of **oppression** for the working classes in several ways. It promises a paradise of eternal bliss in life after death. It makes the present more acceptable by offering compensation and making a virtue of suffering. For example, 'It is easier for a camel to pass through the eye of a needle, than for a rich man to enter the Kingdom of Heaven'.

Marcuse argued that religion oppresses and misleads the working classes by imposing rules and regulations on how they should live their lives. A browbeaten, disciplined working class offers little threat or resistance to the capitalist system. Furthermore, using Marx's theory of **commodity fetishism**, he predicted that as the old gods died, consumerism, aided and abetted by the media, would become the new god. Instead of realising goals for the betterment of society, people begin to worship material goods and mis-recognise themselves in the items they purchase.

3 Weber, in *The Protestant Ethic and the Spirit of Capitalism*, suggested that:

- in some circumstances religion can lead to social change;
- Protestantism helped to produce capitalism.

In opposition to the structural accounts of religion, Weber argued that religion is not always shaped by structural or economic factors. In other words, religion can direct economic development. Central to Weber's analysis was that capitalism developed in areas where Protestantism, or more specifically **Calvinism**, was influential. Weber showed that countries such as India and China had the technological knowledge but lacked a religion that encouraged and facilitated the development of capitalism. Religions such as Hinduism are 'other-worldly' – they stress the escape from the toils of the material world to a higher plane or spiritual existence, whereas Calvinism is a 'salvation' religion – human beings can 'save themselves' if they lead good lives.

Although Calvinism preached a doctrine of predestination, nobody could actually be sure that they were one of the chosen few. Therefore people had to convince themselves that they had been chosen to go to heaven. Working hard and abstaining from over-indulgence produced success in careers. Making money was a concrete indication of success, which instilled confidence that they were destined for heaven. This type of uniform lifestyle is also characteristic of the standardised organisation and reproduction of capitalism (ever-continuing pursuit of profit).

We can also find a number of examples that support Weber's assertion that religion can act as a 'motor' of **social change**. Religion and religious leaders (for example, Martin Luther King and Archbishop Desmond Tutu) have played a central part in revolutionary social movements.

4 Beginning with descriptions of **religious organisations** by **Troeltsch** (1931), we will examine:

- the distinction between **churches, denominations, sects** and **cults**;
- the life cycle of different religious organisations.

Churches tend to be large organisations and, despite their declining influence, are often related to the state as the official religion (for example, Roman Catholicism in the Republic of Ireland). **Denominations** are described as 'diluted' churches (**Stark and Bainbridge**) and although they freely admit new members they do not have the universal appeal that churches have. **Sects** are diametrically opposed to churches – they are smaller and more integrated. According to Troeltsch, they tend to be 'oppositional' (i.e. they reject the values of the world). Members are usually deeply committed to the cause and are asked to opt out of engagement with everyday life.

Wallis offers a framework of understanding religious organisations according to their relationship with the outside world. Firstly, he describes **world-rejecting** new religious movements (**sects**) that have a definite conception of God. Many of these sects are known as **millenarian** movements – they anticipate the intervention of a god who will save their souls and condemn the infidels. Secondly, he describes **world-accommodating** new religious movements (**denominations**). They dispense with elaborate ceremony and offer solace and stimulation for an increasingly secularised personal life. Thirdly, **world-affirming** new religious movements (**cults**) tolerate the existence of other religions. This type of organisation often accepts the world as it appears. They offer the follower the potential to be successful in terms of the dominant values of society by unlocking spiritual powers and offering techniques (for example meditation) that heighten personal awareness and ability.

The growth of sects and cults can be explained in terms of **marginality** (Weber) and **relative deprivation**. For example, those groups of people at the periphery of society who feel they do not share the same rights and privileges as the majority of people may be attracted to certain religious cults or sects. Those who feel relatively deprived in terms of community may be attracted to close-knit religious organisations that offer the fellowship they are yearning for.

Development, organisation and attitude towards the outside world determine the life cycle of sects and cults. For example, it is widely accepted that cults which rely on a charismatic leader cannot survive beyond his or her death. In addition, millenarian movements (who predict the apocalypse) have an inbuilt short life span because if judgement day does not materialise the whole purpose for their existence is undermined.

5 The **secularisation** debate is one which considers two opposing views:

- in Britain, religion is declining in influence;
- the introduction of 'new' religions is proof of religious vitality.

Human progress over the last three centuries has heralded a new era for humankind. The world has been subjected to manipulation and change and scientists appear to be unlocking the great mysteries of life and offering explanations that challenge the very existence of God. Many of the 'great' thinkers (Marx and Durkheim included) argued that the need for religion would wane and be replaced by something else. However, not all thinkers share this belief. **Adorno (Frankfurt School)**, a critic of the Enlightenment, argued that Nazism was the excessive but logical embodiment of humans' control over their environment.

The secularisation issue is an easy one to understand but often difficult to analyse. Fundamentally, it proposes or describes a radical and fundamental change in the institutional foundations of society. **Wilson** suggests that there are three commonly accepted areas that are relevant to this debate. First, there has been a decline in formal religious observance among the Trinitarian churches. Second, there has also been a comparable decline in religious baptisms, confirmations and church marriage. Conversely, the number of civil marriages has risen. Thirdly, the influence of the church as an institution has also significantly decreased. In many ways, it acts as a pressure group, commenting on a variety of secular issues.

Martin describes the secularisation debate as outdated, arguing instead that there is evidence to suggest that religion is thriving. For example, at an individual level it is impossible to ascertain if people have become less religious. Although fewer people go to church, many may still believe in something. Furthermore, he questions the idea that there was once a 'golden age' of religiosity. Were people in Victorian times really more religious?

Through **immigration**, Britain has witnessed the introduction of 'new' religions, which has revitalised the religious debate. Far from declining in significance, religion forms a central part of life for many minority groups – members readily observe formal ritual and practice. Whilst many retain the traditional religious and moral outlook, they also engage as active citizens of a modern (secular) society. On the other hand, their beliefs have brought them into conflict with mainstream sectors of British society. The Rushdie affair, in which the Ayatollah Khomeini issued a *fatwa* (Islamic death sentence) on a British writer, showed that religion was still vital enough to cause much debate and conflict.

30 minutes

Use your knowledge

1. Is religion necessarily a conservative force?

2. Assess the arguments for and against secularisation.

3. How can the organisation of a religion affect its life span?

Mass Media and Popular Culture

5 minutes

Test your knowledge

 1 The _____ _____ analysis of the mass media suggests that it stifles the audience's ability to think freely and critically. Others, using a _____ _____ model, argue that the media can have a negative effect on people.

 2 A number of studies by Bandura, Belson et al have suggested that there is a direct _____ between children watching violent material and committing violent acts.

 3 The discussion of ownership and control has two strands. The _____ model stresses the relationship between ownership and output. The _____ / _____ model argues that it is the economic system that determines the output.

 4 Later research on audiences argues that audiences are _____ rather than _____ . Morley's work shows that the reading of a media text depends on the _____ _____ of the audience.

 5 It is argued that the representations of certain social groups are limited. For example, McRobbie's study of *Jackie* showed that magazines aimed at girls reinforced traditional _____ .

6 The post-modern condition is one that is characterised by _____ . Some theorists celebrate the _____ of mass media, whereas others criticise it for lacking _____ .

Answers

✔ **If you got them all right, skip to page 49**

25 minutes

Improve your knowledge

1 The impact that the mass media has had on modern living cannot be underestimated. Its appeal is global and it cuts through all social divisions. It is ubiquitous, seemingly inescapable. Regarding the term 'mass', readers are reminded not to see it as a pejorative term but think of it as meaning 'reaching many'. The mass media has also been seen from its earliest inception to have the power to cause anti-social behaviour (for example, 'penny dreadfuls') especially amongst the working classes. First, we look at how media content affects audiences.

There are broadly two strands to the **media effects** debate:

- the mass media stifles free and critical thinking;
- the mass media has a negative effect, especially on young audiences.

This approach has been given a number of labels but it is most commonly known as the '**hypodermic needle**' or **conspiracy** theory. The **Frankfurt School** was a collection of scholars who wrote extensively on the impact of the mass media. It is important to understand the context in which they were writing. During the 1930s, Germany had been taken over by the Nazis, whilst American society was experiencing massive immigration and (not necessarily related) social problems (widespread crime and violence). The Frankfurt School cited the rise of the mass media as being instrumental in the rise of Nazism, duping the population into accepting a faulty, quasi-scientific justification of widespread terror, murder and the exploitation of millions of people. Without control of the mass media, the Nazis would not have been able to succeed in winning hearts and minds.

In the United States, the new mass medium of cinema was blamed for leading young impressionable people into immoral, socially unacceptable behaviour. It is worth noting, however, that this cycle of moral panics has always accompanied the mass media – in the 1950s it centred on rock music, in the 1980s 'video nasties', while the 1990s have seen the debate focus on the Internet and video games. (**Cumberbatch** 1993).

Marcuse (*One Dimensional Man*) and **Adorno** (*The Dialectic of the Enlightenment*) also identified another aspect to the 'cultural industries' (mass media), arguing that they stifle people's thinking, because everything is rationalised and repetitive as it is subjected to the same constraints as other profit-making enterprises.

Another theorist linked with the Frankfurt School, **Habermas**, wrote about the displacement/replacement of a genuine '**public sphere**' (free talking amongst equals that determines public opinion and influences governments) by the mass media. The 'public sphere' becomes a sham, swamped by commercialism – it is about forming image rather than rational debate. The crux of this theory is that audiences are not influential but '**passive**' receivers of media messages. This implies the audience is one homogeneous unit, which thinks the same and reacts the same to content. Ultimately, it is a pessimistic and elitist position.

Moral campaigners such as Mary Whitehouse and Gerald Beyer (National Viewers and Listeners Association) still endorse the idea of the 'hypodermic' model. They argue that the media acts as a conspiracy, repeatedly challenging traditional morality.

2 These theories have formed the basis (but not necessarily an ideological basis) of many theoretical/empirical studies. Most research has been concerned mainly with children, because they are seen as more impressionable (easier to manipulate) and watch more television, which may have implications for socialisation. A great deal of research has been content analysis (counting the acts/hours of violence) and has shown that programmes targeted at children are disproportionately more violent than adult programming.

Belson and Eysenck and **Nias** offered psychological explanations suggesting a direct **correlation** between media violence and acts of violence. **Bandura**'s now famous 'bobo doll' study 'proved' that a film with violent content (without moral closure – i.e. the perpetrator was not punished) could influence violent behaviour in children. Belson in his study showed that teenagers who had viewed violent films had committed violent acts. **De Fleur** argued that the media can affect people but it depends on the psychological state of the individual – some are more susceptible than others to persuasion.

However, care should be taken with studies that 'prove' cause and effect. At best, studies and experiments tend to produce contradictory results, which are mainly due to methodological problems. For example, **Belson** relied on the boys' medium-to long-term memories of viewing violence and committing violent acts thereafter. Furthermore, many experiments have taken place in the laboratory rather than in the 'true' environment of the home. However, these findings can be linked with common-sense thinking, in that the media can be implicated in the unquestioning reproduction of common-sense ideas. In reporting the trial of James Bulger's young killers, where the violent film *Child's Play 3* had been implicated, the *Daily Mirror* (November 26, 1993) quoted Clifford, who warned, 'There is no doubt that a constant diet of violence can de-sensitise children to pain and suffering. It is like a constant drip-drip effect – and we should take action to stop it now.' However, there was not any direct proof that the boys had actually watched the film.

The **Glasgow University Media Group** (GUMG) has consistently argued that the media, more specifically the news, is biased towards those in power. In *Bad News*, *More Bad News* and *Really Bad News* they argued that industrial disputes were presented in a selective fashion. Later research by **Greg Philo** (former head of GUMG) in *Seeing Is Believing*, showed through a reconstruction game, that even years after the miners' strike respondents constructed programmes identical to the actual news programmes, which demonstrates the 'ideological power' of such programmes.

3 The issue of **ownership and control** is another central theme in the study of the media. Again, there are two strands to this **conflict model**:

- the **instrumental** model;
- the **structure/determination** approach.

The **instrumental** model is concerned primarily with media ownership and control and its output. The implication of this approach is that the owners (who belong to the ruling class) directly interfere with the outlook and content of the product. Most analysis has focused on newspapers and 'media moguls' (**Turnstall and Palmer** 1991) such as Lord Beaverbrook. Anecdotal evidence shows that in the past, owners directly interfered with the content of the paper. 'I run the Daily Express purely for the purpose of making propaganda, and with no other motive' (*Royal Commission on the Press*, 1949).

The ownership of the media by a small number of people has always worried governments. Rupert Murdoch, in particular, has caused concern with regards to his ever-growing media empire. In addition to his newspaper ownership, he also has interests in satellite broadcasting (BskyB, and Star TV which carried BBC World News), films (20th Century Fox) and book publishing (HarperCollins). Governments try to respond to owners like Rupert Murdoch by constraining cross-media ownership. **Concentration of media output** is seen as detrimental to the fundamentals of democracy (freedom of information) because the media industry does not sell just goods but also 'information' and opinions. For example, Murdoch has courted controversy in his attempts to move into the Asian market. When the Chinese government complained about the BBC's coverage of their activities, Murdoch responded by removing the BBC World Service from the Star television network (which he owns and controls). It is alleged that he also blocked Chris Patten's memoirs from being published because Patten was highly critical of the handover of Hong Kong to China.

In addition, up until 1997, Murdoch's political leanings were never in doubt. After a savage attack on Neil Kinnock and Labour's **1992 election** campaign, the *Sun* printed the headline, 'It's the Sun wot (sic) won it'. The political stance of most British newspapers was fervently anti-Labour (pro-Conservative) and many commentators argued that this attitude entered the public's consciousness. In support of this analysis, Goldsmith's Media Research Group argued that erroneous 'loony left' council stories (for example, about left-wing councils banning 'Baa Baa Black Sheep' for being racist) distracted electors from the 'real' issues of the campaign. The media can also set the agenda by focusing on issues which may or may not be a political party's traditional strengths. It has been argued that the Labour victory in 1997 can be partly accounted for by media interest in issues such as the NHS.

However, care should be taken when using the ownership question in isolation. As Turnstall and Palmer point out, 'Media moguldom is only one important aspect of a … media industry of almost endless complexity' (1991).

The **structure/determination** approach echoes the Frankfurt School's assertion that it is capitalism that determines the form and content of the mass media. It is the economic, organisational and cultural climate in which the media industries operate that either creates or limits opportunities for industry owners. In other words, owners have to react to market constraints by responding to audiences to maximise profits. The strategy of profit-maximisation has led to the following trends. First, the **concentration of ownership** (as predicted by Marx) allows owners a 'free hand' at maximising audiences and limiting the breadth of output. Second, media markets have become '**internationalised**' in the search for new markets. Third, the trend has been for media companies to spread their risks. This has resulted in diversification into **cross-media ownership**. This takes two forms: **horizontal**, which is achieved by taking over a competitor, and **vertical**, which means buying a 'link' in the production chain (for example, taking over a software company to provide products for your hardware).

Decision-making has to be placed in an economic and political context. For example, it can be argued that journalists and editors, although autonomous, are agents of the ruling class's ideology and interests; they will adopt the taken-for-granted attitudes (representations of certain groups) or assumptions that support the status quo. This can manifest itself in the actual construction of media texts. For example, where news stories involve industrial relations, research has shown that there is often bias against employees and unions through presentation and selection of events.

The **market/liberal-democratic** model, in stark contrast to the conflict model detailed above, regards media output as a result of supply and demand – consumers create output. The wide range of media products suggests that a whole variety of consumers are being catered for. Furthermore, if there is no demand a product will not be produced.

However, in reality media markets are not as perfectly competitive as this model suggests. The media industry is experiencing increasing concentration of ownership. In addition, the idea behind public service broadcasting (also known as **liberal paternalism**) is that the market does not and cannot provide everything. The state has intervened to uphold general standards and quality.

 The essence of this approach is to look at the media in terms of what people do with the media rather than what the media does to people. It is argued that the audience is **active** rather than **passive**.

Katz and Lazarsfeld's **two-step flow** model rejected the 'hypodermic syringe' model, arguing that when it comes to voting, opinion leaders and other environmental factors are more influential on the audience than the output of the media.

The work of **McQuail, Blumer and Brown** has been influential in the changing approach towards the media debate. They argued that the media satisfies different needs, which can be **informational** (news acting as surveillance of the world), offer **companionship** (sympathising/empathising/interacting with characters in soap operas), **escapist** (fantasy, dreamlike) or purely **entertainment** (quiz shows). This change in approach emphasised the active consumer over the passive. Despite being a rather dated theory, its relevance may be significant in what some thinkers refer to as the post-modern realm.

Morley (*Nationwide Audience,* 1980), using **Hall**'s **encoding/decoding** model, argued that the social characteristics of the audience (occupation, ethnicity) determined the 'decoding' (reading of the text). The 'encoding' is the process of putting together the actual programme itself. Hall theorised that media professionals carry with them a number of assumptions and ways of doing things. For instance, most programme makers are male, white and middle class and the output will reflect that. Morley wanted to test Hall's hypothesis by finding out how audiences decoded *Nationwide*, a news magazine programme that followed the main news on BBC1.

He found that bank managers and unskilled manual workers actually gave the same **preferred reading** of the news programmes. In other words, they agreed with the value-consensus interpretation of events. This is because the bank managers had a professional outlook which was shared with media professionals. On the other hand, unskilled workers, due to their education (or lack of it) and lack of exposure to discussion of such matters, did not have the required knowledge to offer a critical analysis.

He showed that students often offered a **negotiated reading**, which can be described as both agreeing and disagreeing with the programme's version of events. For example, they showed an awareness of how news stories were 'constructed'.

Morley found that trades union officials and black students were more likely to take an **oppositional reading**, arguing that the media is biased and works in favour of the dominant ideology. They therefore disagreed with and challenged the presentation of facts. Their backgrounds and life experiences were not conducive to accepting the presentation of facts.

In Morley's work *Family Television*, he showed that viewing can often be the site of a power struggle over who watches what (who is in possession of the remote control) and that this is related to gender and economic power. **Silverstone** also advocated that ethnographic research on television consumption should take place in the 'naturalistic laboratory' of the home.

Other research in the **cultural studies** tradition has focused on what meanings are derived from different types of programmes. For example, **Ang and Hobson** have shown how female viewers identify and get emotionally involved with the fortunes of soap opera characters, linking them with their own experiences in life (for example, suggesting possible solutions for problems).

5 By discussing **representations**, the tendency is for researchers to focus on how the media reinforces the consensual view of the world. This section will focus on the representations of:

- **ethnicity**;
- **sex/gender**;
- **deviance**.

Hartman and Husband and **Hiro** look at how the media always provides 'a framework for thinking' about race relations. In other words, 'race' (or ethnicity) equals problems. Although it could be argued that there is more sensitivity today, comedy programmes from the 1960s and 1970s (such as *Love Thy Neighbour, Rising Damp,* and *Mind Your Language*) and more 'serious' programming regarding non-white people have concentrated on immigration controls, racial discrimination and legislation. Hartman and Husband describe this as a consequence of the 'imperialist legacy' of British culture, where the media employs **stereotypes** of black people that reflect white people's shared imperialistic 'hangover' and associate dark skin pigmentation with dirt, poverty and low social status. Also, the arrival of new immigrants is often described as a 'flood', which has negative connotations.

McRobbie, in her study of *Jackie*, shows how girls' magazines reinforced traditional stereotypes of females. Stories often focused on the need to be attractive and falling in love. **Ferguson**, in a very similar vein, showed in her study of women's magazines that self-improvement (self-discipline through and for consumerism) and 'getting your man' are top of the agenda. **Van Zoonen** in her analysis showed that women are under-represented in news. If they are shown, they are often seen in domestic surroundings or offering emotional eyewitness accounts. **Tuchmann** argued that women are '**symbolically annihilated**' by their absence from the public sphere, and often condemned or trivialised when they enter into it (for example, the widespread negative reporting of the Greenham Common protesters by newspapers).

Ditton and Duffy found an over-reporting of violent and sex crimes, even though they make up a very small percentage of all crimes, and noted that sensationalism helps instill a fear of crime. **Hall**, in *Policing the Crisis*, argued that the media reinforced ideological views on law and order. In other words, they shifted focus from a crisis of capitalism itself to blaming others for the crisis, i.e. young black men (and immigrant labour, which was seen as surplus labour). This also relates to the section on 'ethnicity'. **Cohen**'s *Folk Devils and Moral Panics* showed how the 'riots' of the 1960s were in fact minor disturbances, but adverse media coverage exacerbated the extent of these disturbances and more people decided to attend. This is known as **deviance amplification**.

 The advent of new technology has led to **globalisation** and to what people describe as the **post-modern realm**. As a result we have witnessed:

- fundamental changes in how we live;
- certainty being replaced by **uncertainty**.

There is a notion that the world has become one 'global village' (Ted Turner) through the growth of the media and communications networks. The compression of space and time (see **Harvey**, *The Condition of Postmodernity*, and **Thompson**, *Media and Modernity*) allows people in one part of the world to be connected with others elsewhere, instantaneously. An event happening in one part of the world can be witnessed by millions of others at the same time; people can transcend barriers and borders by communicating with one another via radio, telephone or the Internet. Because of these global links, we live in a very different world today – our patterns of communication and sociability have changed.

Some theorists, namely **Baudrillard** and **Jameson**, describe this as the post-modern realm. For Baudrillard, the mass media has changed the very nature of our lives – it defines our world. He uses the term **hyperreality** to describe real events becoming indistinguishable from their images (e.g. events such as the Gulf War becoming television events). These images form part of the framework of our lives and behaviour – the images define and fashion how we make sense of the world.

The **post-modern condition** is celebrated and rebuked at the same time. Whilst theorists celebrate the uncertainty, emphasising the democratisation/liberalisation and **playfulness** of individual identities and media texts that exemplify the post-modern condition, others take a more critical view, arguing that form has overtaken substance. **Jameson** in particular describes post-modern forms as pastiche ('death of the author') – in other words, people have run out of ideas and originality. The re-mix of the Police song 'Every Breath You Take' by Puff Daddy would be severely criticised as symptomatic of the post-modern condition. It is wholesale copying without any criticism – i.e. pastiche.

McRobbie, on the other hand, celebrates post-modern culture, describing how young people borrow elements from different cultures and actually invent their own looks. This 'look' does not belong to a particular time and place, and there are several of these 'looks' at any one time. Exposure to a world via the global media allows audiences access to different cultures from around the world to 'pick and mix' from as they wish.

However, critics such as **Turnstall** argue that the globalisation of culture is actually **American cultural imperialism**. Despite people becoming more individualised (a mark of post-modernism) by picking and choosing different lifestyles, the globalisation of the media has developed unevenly. It is predominantly American (or anglophonic) media products that are being exported to the rest of the world. At the same time, American values and culture and the material trappings that accompany them are also conveyed. Societies, therefore are importing (or adopting) an 'American' way of life, which may also act as a platform for American companies to forge (or exploit) new markets.

30 minutes

Use your knowledge

1 'It's not what the media does to people, it's what people do with the media that counts.' How true is this statement?

2 Is ownership and control of the media important?

3 Discuss the representations in the media of two social groups.

5 minutes

 **Test** your knowledge

1 The fact that health and illness are not equally distributed amongst all people suggests that they may be socially _____ .

2 Functionalists describe illness as _____ to society because it renders people incapable of contributing fully to society. The role of health professionals is to restore individuals to a fully _____ role. Marxists view health care as a subsidy. In addition, Navarro contends that health care is treated as a _____ like any other to be bought and sold. Interactionism is interested in how patients _____ their health care with doctors.

3 Left-wing thinking proposes that a _____ in poverty would result in a _____ in poor health. Right-wing theorists argue that higher incidences of certain illnesses can be found in the lower classes because they _____ choose less healthy lifestyles.

4 Certain illnesses are sex-specific, but there are discrepancies in non-specific illnesses such as lung cancer. This can be attributed to the different _____ of men and women.

5 Figures show that members of the Afro-Caribbean and Asian communities in Britain are more likely to be diagnosed as _____ . This may be attributed to the social and cultural bias of psychiatrists.

6 Statistics show that the _____ of England has higher rates of mortality than the _____ .

7 In Goffman's analysis of mental illness, he argues that once a person is _____ as mentally ill, that label stays with him or her for life.

Answers

 If you got them all right, skip to page 56

25 minutes

Improve your knowledge

1 The body, according to scientific and biological discourse, is analogous to a machine (GPs' surgeries advertise 'patient MOT' clinics) and like a car, if it malfunctions or breaks down (physically or mentally) it is subjected to repair by health professionals (or body mechanics). The accepted pedagogy of mainstream biomedical practice is to treat illness by **allopathic** means (prescribing medicines, antibiotics, etc.). However, this rather narrow and mechanistic view of the body proposes that illness is purely a natural phenomenon. Whilst death and bouts of illness seem to be indisputable facts of life, health and illness can also be considered as **social constructs**.

Contemporary sociological thinking about health and illness, therefore, moves beyond the 'natural' realm of biomedicine and tries to explain why some people are likely to be healthier or more prone to illness than others. For example, anorexia, which can be described as both a mental and a physical condition, is unheard-of in countries ravaged by poverty and famine, in which malnutrition, starvation and death are everyday encounters. However, in relatively affluent countries, anorexia is a well-known, much-discussed and publicised condition. This supports the assertion that illness is socially constructed (in the case of anorexia, the representations of the female form in the mass media have been implicated). Likewise, variations in health and illness can be found in different social groups (based on class, gender, region and ethnicity).

One only has to look at the changing nature of the ideal body type in different historical times to understand the ambiguity of what it means to be healthy and desirable. **Foucault**'s notion of '**technological bodies**' links the biomedical with the social, arguing that our bodies can now become something that we create or control through dieting, training programmes and surgery. Indeed, biomedical advances are moving the body as a natural 'machine' to a site of biological and social control. We can now prevent or delay natural occurrences (e.g. pregnancy) by following a prescribed course of action (e.g. contraception). The logical extension of control is to configure or pre-programme the human body with certain characteristics. Whilst research is concentrating on how to eliminate illnesses and disabilities that are genetically inherited, for many critics, the movement into some areas of **genetic engineering** and the possibility of selecting certain (desirable) physical attributes in children seems insidious (and is linked by some to Nazi

Germany's eugenics programme). It raises new moral dilemmas about how much control and choice should be exercised and by whom.

The **functionalist** account sees illness as **dysfunctional** to society in that it renders people incapable of properly contributing to society. Health organisations like the NHS help restore or re-adjust the individual (who sought their help) into a fully **functional** role, which is beneficial to society as a whole. Furthermore, **Parsons** argues that the professional monopoly on the administration of drugs and medicine held by doctors (who are professionally obliged to conduct themselves according to the 'Hippocratic oath') is a necessary and desirable arrangement of health provision.

In contrast, the **Marxist** position, articulated primarily by **Navarro**, argues that health provisions (like the NHS) are inextricably linked with the economic system. Doctors act as agents of social control, to keep the workforce healthy. In other words, the state is subsidising capitalism – a healthy workforce is a productive workforce. Although health care may have very real benefits to individuals, it is described as a concession, which masks the exploitative nature of the social and economic arrangements. For **Althusser**, the NHS operates as an **Ideological State Apparatus** (ISA) by creating the illusion of a 'caring' (capitalist) society. **Hall**, using **Gramsci**'s notion of **'hegemony'**, explains how the state strikes a deal by providing services to the working classes, in return for which the state is granted legitimacy. As long as these 'common-sense' measures are maintained (i.e. people can receive health care when it is required) the inevitable crisis in capitalism is delayed.

Health is also a **commodity** to be bought and sold like any other item. **Marx** predicted an inexorable drive towards the monopolisation of the economy. The announcement of the merger of Glaxo Wellcome and SmithKline Beecham in January 2000 (capturing 7% of the global market) is just one example of the pharmaceutical industry showing this trend. Navarro argues that the **concentration of ownership** by multinational companies does not benefit the majority of people (especially those in Third World countries). The *Guardian*'s Duncan Campbell wryly pointed out that if it was discovered that aspirin cured AIDS its price would multiply by one million overnight.

A good starting point for **interactionism** is to ask the following questions. What are health and illness? How are they interpreted from one individual to another? The work of **Zola** and **Rosenhan** focuses on negotiation and relationships between patient and doctor. They show that variables such as class, gender, age, ethnicity and medical history will have an impact on the diagnosis and subsequent treatment or non-treatment. Recent studies on cancer therapy have shown that middle class patients tend to **negotiate** better and quicker treatments than working class patients. Many factors can be attributed to this success. Many middle-class patients will be able effectively to communicate their symptoms more articulately or 'correctly' and so will be on more equal terms with the middle-class doctor. In addition, middle-class people are more likely to have private health cover and their relationship with the doctor is not just as patient but as fee-paying customer.

3 It is well documented that middle-class patients negotiate and utilise a broader range of services than working-class patients do. However, research shows that lower-class people, at whatever life stage, are more likely to fall ill or die than middle-class people. For some scholars, these figures cannot just be attributed to the lack of negotiation skills of the lower classes. Left-wing thinkers, such as **Doyal** and **Navarro**, argue that a reduction in ill health would follow a reduction in social and economic inequality. This was echoed by the *Inequalities of Health* report (1979) which concluded that the conditions of poverty (lack of knowledge, lack of money, poor housing) were the main factors contributing to poor health. For example, the diet of the less well off is reliant on cheap processed food, whose nutritional value is reduced during manufacture. Unfortunately, the more 'natural' and fresh produce is generally more expensive and out of the budget of many lower-class families. Therefore, poorer people are more at risk of dying of those diseases that are associated with inferior quality food consumption than affluent people. In many cases, however, people suffering from illness may enter a situation where ill health actually affects social class (by not being able to attend work), which becomes a cyclical process because the lack of resources associated with being unemployed (to ensure a good diet, for example) worsens the problem. Furthermore, it is difficult, considering the inevitability of employers wanting healthy workers, for the sick and poor to obtain and keep good jobs and escape the conditions in which they find themselves.

Cultural variations and lifestyle choices of different people can also explain differences in levels of health and illness. As **Bourdieu** shows, these lifestyle choices (for example, diet, smoking and drinking) can influence health. For example, in *Distinctions* (1983) Bourdieu identified patterns of '**class consumption**', in which he describes the working class preference for economic, filling food (which is high in calories and carbohydrates) as arising out of necessity to cheaply reproduce labour power or 'a forced choice produced by conditions of existence which rule out all alternatives… and leave no choice but the taste of the necessary' (1983). This becomes an emblem of class 'they bear in their very bodies'. On the other hand, those who are 'distanced from necessity' (the middle classes) have a different awareness and interest in self-presentation and choose to eat less fattening foods. Middle-class women, whose appearance contributes to their occupational value, not only have the money but an interest in dieting (buying the best food) and beautification. According to Bourdieu, this explains why as one moves down the social hierarchy the waist measurement of women increases.

However, less sympathetic theorists argue that individual lifestyles are best understood as a **voluntary choice** rather than a result of social or cultural circumstances. They point to the high incidence of smoking in the working classes and argue that individuals still have a choice in how they live their life. The high rates of cancer amongst working class people can be attributed to choices, which are borne out in statistics which showed that 34% of manual workers smoked compared with 22% of non-manual workers (Department of Health 1996). This problem is further exacerbated by the 'dependency culture' of the welfare state, which protects people from the consequences of their own actions.

4 Obviously, certain illnesses and diseases are sex-specific (e.g. cervical and testicular cancer), but the fact that there are huge discrepancies between men and women developing illnesses which are not sex-specific, such as lung cancer, suggests that those differences can be attributed to the **different lifestyles of men and women**. Historically, men have been more likely to smoke and drink than women (the mean weekly consumption of alcohol for men was 16 units, whereas women consumed 6.3 units – Department of Health 1996) which may account for why, on average, women are expected to live longer than men. As social taboos on women smoking and drinking recede, the trend of more women indulging in these activities suggests that future incidences of alcohol- and tobacco-related illnesses in women may rise. However, in the face of this, a contributory factor to a longer life expectancy for women is that they are more likely to take precautionary action by visiting a doctor more frequently than men. A recent governmental testicular cancer awareness campaign focused on men's general lack of health awareness and their reluctance to carry out self-examination and encouraged them to visit the doctor for regular check-ups.

5 **Ethnicity** cannot be disentangled from class. Any analysis of ethnicity has to consider the socio-economic factors, and many ethnic minorities tend to occupy lower-paid jobs and poor housing and have poorer diets (i.e. nutritionally deficient). There are no real patterns of health and illness that are wholly determined by ethnicity. However, figures suggest that Afro-Caribbeans and Asians are more likely to be diagnosed as **schizophrenic**. Mental illness, as discussed below, can be viewed as a social construct and it has been suggested that the stress of being a member of a minority social/ethnic group may be a contributory factor. However, psychiatric diagnosis is not a pure science and the higher proportion of schizophrenics from ethnic minorities may reflect the institutional, social and cultural bias of white, middle class psychiatrists.

6 Different **regions** have different mortality rates, and it has been shown that the **north** of England has higher mortality rates than the **south** (for example, from heart disease). Again, regional differences cannot be separated from class and the figures may reflect the traditional structural conditions of the north (poorer conditions, poorer households and neighbourhoods). Indeed, it may also reflect the historical differences in health care provision. For example, treatment for breast cancer has been described as a 'national lottery', as survival rates vary from region to region.

7 In many cases, a physical illness is an indisputable fact and can be located and treated accordingly. Mental illness, on the other hand, is not as apparent as this and theorists are interested in explaining how mental illness is constructed. **Foucault** concentrated on how mental health and madness were differently constructed at different times – what is deemed normal and abnormal behaviour has altered over time. For Foucault, the '**medicalisation of madness**' (i.e. scientific understanding) is essentially an oppressive discourse, which has been used by those in power as a justification of incarcerating and punishing people rather than actually helping them.

Psychiatric **labels** are pejorative in the same way that the label 'AIDS sufferer' has been. The mentally ill are stigmatised and the diagnosis of being mentally ill often stays with an individual (cured or not) for life. **Rosenhan and Goffman**'s research (1978) has shown that even normal patterns of behaviour are interpreted according to the label given to the person (a **self-fulfilling prophecy**). In some cases, the note-taking and data collection of pseudo-patients (who were really researchers) in mental institutions was seen as symptomatic of their condition.

30 minutes

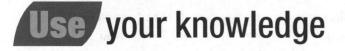
Use your knowledge

 What sociological explanations are given for different levels of health and illness in different social groups?

 Compare and contrast the functionalist and Marxist accounts of healthcare provision.

3 Evaluate the interactionist contribution to the sociology of health.

5 minutes

Test your knowledge

 1 Functionalism stresses the importance of _____ and _____ between different workers. Marxism describes work as an _____ relationship.

 2 Standardised working practices, known as _____ , have been replaced by a new set of arrangements known as _____ , which is characterised by _____ working practices, _____ hierarchies and a more _____ skilled workforce.

 3 Marx argued that workers become _____ from the practice of work. Later Marxist thinkers have argued that new work practices have led to _____ . Goldthorpe and Lockwood show that workers take an _____ view to employment, choosing higher earnings so they may pursue activities outside work.

 4 Functionalists argue that industrial action is _____ for society, whereas Marxists believe that conflict is _____ . Dahrendorf suggest that unions have _____ conflict, handing workers some autonomy. However, Hyman describes a _____ _____ phase in Britain in the late 1970s and 1980s, when the Conservative government subjected unions to a number of attacks.

 5 There is disagreement on how unemployment figures are compiled. Right-wing critics describe figures as an _____ , whereas critics of the previous Conservative administration accused it of _____ by changing the definition of unemployment over 30 times.

6 Parker identifies three patterns of leisure. The _____ pattern is typical of highly paid professionals. The _____ pattern is characteristic of those professions that want to keep work and leisure separate, whereas the _____ pattern describes leisure as an escape.

 **Answers**

1 interdependence, co-operation, exploitative **2** Fordism, post-Fordism, flexible, flatter, diversely **3** alienated, de-skilling, instrumental **4** dysfunctional, inevitable, institutionalised, coercive pacification **5** overestimation, underestimation **6** extension, neutrality, opposition

✔ **If you got them all right, skip to page 65**

Improve your knowledge

1 Work and economic life

Arguably, work and the **mass interdependence of organisations** (which structure our working lives) are central and inevitable features of contemporary living. For many people, work is dull and repetitive but a 'necessary evil' in the cyclical production and reproduction of goods and services. The duties we have to perform each day dictate a considerable proportion of our lives – they are pivotal to our social experience. Work has social significance; it gives direction and we bring to it and take away a whole range of diverse meanings, needs and desires. We are workers and consumers at the same time; we have to play because 'consumerism is the only game in town'.

Modern industrial capitalist societies demand that we must work to exchange our wages for goods and services in order to live. Attitudes towards work are **historically specific**. The work ethic celebrated by today's society reflects the religious, philosophical and moral tenets of **Calvinism**: to work hard is to be virtuous; to be lazy is derided. Popular right-of-centre discourses (articulated annually at political party conferences and in the popular press) echo Weber's description of the Protestant ethic by focusing on 'dole scroungers' (implying that those who are fit and able to work should work).

If this state of affairs worsened, i.e. a considerable proportion of the population ceased contributing to the economy, it would be dysfunctional to a system which relies on the interdependence of different organisations (large and small) with individuals using different skills. This system needs a commitment by most, if not all, people for the greater good. Central to **functionalist** analysis is that the 'unwritten contract' of **co-operation** (learnt in families and schools) is recognised to benefit the individual, whose hard work ensures their company's success (and the economy's), which in turn safeguards their employment. If the social contract is broken, for example through self-interest (not wanting to work), this may undermine the fabric of society. If some individuals opt out but benefit from the system, people may question why these individuals should be able to live off the hard work of others.

The **Marxists**, on the other hand, concentrate on the **exploitative** relationship between the bourgeoisie (ruling class), who own and control the means of production, and the proletariat (working class) who, out of stark economic necessity, have to sell their labour in order to survive. It is an exploitative relationship because the labourer never receives the full value of his or her work, whilst the owner, in pursuit of profit, retains the surplus value (the difference between the wage that was paid to the labourer and the amount received by the employer for the goods or services). Other Marxists (such as **Marcuse** in *One Dimensional Man*), using Marx's notion of **commodity fetishism**, argue that the working classes enslave themselves to the chains of capitalism by desiring goods and services (a new car, the latest television, etc.) produced by the very system that exploits them.

2 The changing nature and organisation of work from Fordism to post-Fordism

One of the major issues regarding the sociology of work is that the nature of work has moved from **Fordist** principles of organisation to **post-Fordism**. The term Fordism is inspired by the adoption by the Ford car company of the scientific principle of dividing work into small separate tasks (also known as Taylorism) to mass manufacture the Ford Model T car. A strict method of work was imposed where workers, working to the speed of the production line, specialised in assembling just one part of the car. The core feature of the Fordist production line, which was adopted by many other manufacturers, is **standardisation** – fixed production lines, hierarchies and bureaucracies (which Weber described as a necessary feature of modern living).

However, theorists such as **Piore** and **Sabel** argued that capitalism, facilitated by new technology (global communication networks and micro-processing computing technology), is undergoing a metamorphosis. The proponents of this change argue that the very nature of capitalism is moving the emphasis away from strict hierarchies, inflexible working practices, and workers with limited skills towards **flatter hierarchies, flexible working practices** and a more **diversely skilled** workforce (who own a 'portfolio' of skills). For instance, the **post-Fordist** (global) economy can be characterised by companies utilising computer technology to re-program machinery and accommodate demands for small production runs. Likewise, workers move from one job to another, developing and utilising a multitude of skills.

Whilst this may seem the perfect antidote to the de-personalising and alienating production line, many theorists (for example, **Harvey**) depart from Piore and

Sabel's optimism, arguing that the post-Fordist condition is one that breeds uncertainty and job losses. The 'core' workers (skilled craftspeople) may benefit from these 'new' arrangements by intellectually engaging and testing their skills in a diverse range of tasks, but for the 'peripheral' workers flexibility is characterised by moving from one badly-paid, unsatisfying job (or what 'temping' agencies call assignment) to another. Far from enjoying the new democratic equal relationship with management, they are subjected to **greater control and surveillance**.

Theorists such as **Pollert** contest whether Fordism has actually been eclipsed by a new era of work practices and organisation. The notion that Fordism is a monolithic and inflexible arrangement is a questionable one because companies have always relied on hiring and firing extra 'casual' labour according to production demands. Furthermore, many companies have always been geared up for small production runs. To insist that post-Fordist companies (who have a tendency to merge and concentrate markets) produce more individual goods than their predecessors may be seen as a little premature and over-celebratory.

3 Alienation and work satisfaction

For **Marx**, workers are automatically **alienated** from their work if they do not own or exercise control over what is produced. The act of work, according to Marx, should be an expressive, fulfilling, world-improving activity, but this can never be realised within the structures of capitalism. As a consequence, work is an exploitative, miserable and unsatisfying activity. Relations are not based on human value but market value. People become commodities like any other, to be bought and sold. **Braverman**, using Marx's concept of alienation, argues that the 20th century has born witness to the degradation of work. The implementation of new technologies and work practices has had a double effect. Firstly, workers are **de-skilled**, which denies them the opportunity of gaining complete knowledge of the whole manufacturing process. Secondly, the outcome is that the workforce is easier to control because it is more difficult for it to offer resistance against employers.

In contrast to this all-embracing Marxist position, **Blauner** develops the argument that technology increases alienation. Blauner asserts that alienation is subjective (to each individual) and depends on how new technology has impacted on people's occupations. It is argued that workers who make a genuine, identifiable contribution to the final product or gain increased responsibility feel less alienated (or more satisfied) than those in occupations that have been reduced to mere machine minding.

Goldthorpe and Lockwood's study of Luton car workers refutes the Marxist assertion that workers are passive, miserable robots in the workplace, arguing that workers often bring their own meanings (motivations) into the workplace. They showed that workers who entered well-paid production-line work had an **instrumental** approach to their work. Far from being detached by their alienation, they actually chose to be alienated – it is a means to an end. Work allowed them to pursue leisure interests and fulfilment in the domestic sphere.

4 Conflict at work

For **Marxists**, it is not social consensus but **conflict** that forms the basis of relations in capitalist society. Conflict at work is hardly surprising considering capitalism's exploitative nature and inherent contradictions. In principle, the union consciousness of the working classes is applauded because it stresses a collective identity. However, unions do not fundamentally challenge the structures of capitalism but win concessions. This serves the interests of the system (for example, health and safety laws may protect members but dilute the true horror of capitalism). Unions can also be divisive by pitching members of the working classes against one another (for example, unions often fight to keep a parity of earnings with those who are paid less). For Marxists, the reality is that the workers are all in the same position and have a common interest in overthrowing the system rather than fighting against one another.

A **functionalist** response to industrial conflict and those groups which initiate disruptive action (in which millions of working days are lost) is that they undermine the social obligation of working towards a common goal. However, deviance can be functional if, for instance, strike action has led to better and safer working practices. This is close to the **pluralist** account, articulated primarily by **Dahrendorf**, who argues that the unionisation of labour has **institutionalised** conflict, offering greater stability to industrial relations as a whole. In this context, the activities of unions (who may resort to strikes and other forms of industrial action) are seen as normal and progressive, as the balance of power in the workplace is contested.

Industrial action, usually initiated by unions representing their members' interests, can take many forms (strikes, working to rule, overtime bans) and have many reasons. In Britain in 1993, 60% of days lost to strike action were lost because of disputes about planned redundancies, whereas in 1996 (a time of economic recovery) 80% of disputes were about pay. More recently, in 1999, unions at the Ford Cowley plant called a strike to protest against racism on the shop floor.

Conflict, as shown by Walton and Young, can also be initiated by individuals who have resorted to industrial sabotage, sometimes out of boredom. In the 1980s, there was an erosion of union power by Margaret Thatcher's Conservative government through a number of acts of parliament. **Hyman** describes this as the **coercive pacification phase**. Unemployment and the restructuring of the economy (especially the loss of traditional manufacturing industries that had high levels of union membership) also weakened union power.

 ### Unemployment (gender, ethnic and age differences)

The mid- 1980s and early 1990s in Britain can be contrasted as having the highest and lowest rates of unemployment since World War II. However, controversy still rages over how unemployment statistics are compiled, some arguing that the true rate is **overestimated** because it includes those who will not work rather than those who cannot, whereas others argue that it is **underestimated**. Critics of the Conservative administration of the 1980s and 1990s argue that the definition of unemployment was changed so many times (over 30) to manipulate and hide the real rate of unemployment.

Post-war **Keynesian** policies of aiming for full employment kept unemployment at relatively low levels. However, by the 1970s, what Habermas described as a **legitimation crisis** was brought about by an oil crisis (where fuel costs increased by 400%), recession (high unemployment and inflation) and consequently social and economic instability. Governments moved away from the apparent 'failure' of Keynesian policies of demand management to **monetarist** policies of controlling the money supply and thus inflation, preferring the market rather than the state to find the true market level of unemployment (according to demand). The 1980s and 1990s can be marked as a period of transition. The changes in economic policy were also coupled with other movements, such as globalisation (increased competition from around the world), de-industrialisation and the introduction of new technologies in the work place, which all had a huge impact on unemployment levels.

Unemployment affects many different types of people but does not hit all workers equally. The most likely group to be unemployed is the lower social classes – those employed in non-skilled manual labour. Furthermore, people belonging to ethnic minority groups and aged between 16 and 24 (particularly people of Afro-Caribbean, Pakistani and Bangladeshi origin) are more than twice as likely to be unemployed as their white counterparts. These figures can be attributed to racist and stereotypical attitudes held by employers (also known as 'institutional racism'), which further exacerbate other problems that typically come about from holding a lower class position.

Unemployment is cited as having multiple effects on the individual and society as a whole. Obviously, the loss of financial security and the risk of getting into debt is one consequence, but it can have disastrous consequences for family life, party due to the stress of being poor. **Fagin and Little** found that unemployed people lose a sense of identity and purpose in life. The increase in benefit payments to the unemployed adds an extra burden on treasury finances – money that was to have been spent elsewhere (e.g. on the NHS) may have to be redirected. Unemployment also puts those who remain employed in a state of fear and uncertainty. This 'culture of fear' traps people (for the sake of security) in jobs and occupations they are unhappy with.

Women are less likely to be unemployed than men, but this may be a reflection of social security rules, which prevent married women from independently claiming benefits. Women are also more likely to be employed in lower-paid part-time work, although the number of women entering full-time employment increased in the late 1990s. Despite the 1990 Equal Opportunities Act, women are paid on average less than men and occupy fewer managerial positions. In many situations, women are confronted by the prejudices of (predominantly) male employers and managers. It is assumed that women will take a career break to have children (taking full responsibility for their upbringing) and they are discriminated against as a consequence. In many cases where women have had a break from work, they return to occupations that have lower status and lower pay.

6 Leisure

Work and leisure are seen as diametrically opposed, but it is often work that dictates leisure patterns. **Parker** identified three patterns. First, there is the **extension** pattern where there is not a clear distinction between work and leisure. This pattern is usually found in occupations that are usually highly rewarding. For example, the golf course is often the extension of the boardroom. Second, Parker proposes a **neutrality** pattern, in which work and leisure are two distinct spheres – they are organised separately from one another. Thirdly, he identifies an **opposition** pattern, where leisure becomes an escape from the humdrum routine of work.

A **conflict** perspective on leisure can take two forms. Some theorists argue that people mis-recognise themselves in the commodities with which they surround themselves (**Marcuse**), whilst others, like **Hoch** (1972), use a 'sedative' model, arguing that the mass media and sporting events in particular have replaced religion as the 'new opiate of the masses'.

It should be noted that although women and men have very similar leisure patterns in the home, on average, men are more likely to engage in sport than women are (1995). Men are also more likely to engage in activities outside the home. This can be explained in two ways. On the first count, **Brownmiller** argued that women are controlled by men through the fear of attack or unwanted attention from men in the public sphere. On the other hand, **gender socialisation** positions males and females from birth, through toys and play and in the way they are spoken to. Males are encouraged to be active, whereas females are 'domesticated', which may have an effect on the way each group pursues different activities later on in life.

30 minutes

 Use your knowledge

1 Describe and account for the changes in work practices over the last 30 years.

2 How do functionalist and Marxist accounts of work differ?

3 Why did unemployment increase in the 1980s?

Education

Test your knowledge

1 According to functionalists, the role of education is to socialise children into the _____ and _____ of society.

2 The Marxists Bowles and Gintis argue that the education system produces obedient, docile and highly motivated workers. This is also known as the ' _____ _____ '.

3 Ivan Illich proposes in his book _____ _____ that schooling is unnecessary and harmful. Instead he suggests ' _____ _____ ', where everyday skills are taught by everyday ' _____ '.

4 The social democratic position proposes that educational success can be achieved with the intervention of the _____ .

5 The interactionist perspective concentrates on how teachers and pupils interact. They use the term _____ - _____ _____ . In other words, if teachers believe that pupils will do well they are more likely to achieve academic success.

6 Bourdieu argues that middle class children do better than working class children because they possess _____ _____ which can be converted into educational success.

7 Bernstein argues that middle class children have a distinct advantage because they communicate in the same speech patterns as the school. Educational institutions communicate using an _____ _____ . Working class children are more likely to use a _____ _____ .

8 Feminists contend that the curriculum and educational literature is sexist, placing _____ knowledge and experiences above _____ .

9 The change in government policy, linking education with the economy, is also known as the _____ _____ .

Answers

1 norms, values 2 hidden curriculum 3 *Deschooling Society*, skill exchanges, experts 4 state 5 self-fulfilling prophecy 6 cultural capital 7 elaborated code, restricted code 8 men's, women's 9 new vocationalism

 **If you got them all right, skip to page 77**

66

25 minutes

Improve your knowledge

1 According to the **functionalist** perspective of **Durkheim**, education has a dual role:

- schools teach children **specific skills** for future occupations;
- schools are responsible for the transmission of society's **norms and values** – they emphasise co-operation and commitment to a single 'bigger' cause.

In pre-industrial societies, skills were passed down from one generation to another; educational organisations emerged in response to the needs of industrialisation. The impersonal and complex organisational nature of modern societies demands that workers are, at the very least, literate and numerate. Furthermore, education responds to the different demands of technology and work (consider the emphasis placed on IT in schools and colleges today). Functionalist analysis also argues that complex societies rely on the interdependence of skills, on co-operation and on the solidarity of different individuals. Education, therefore, is responsible for developing a sense of commitment to others (for example, acquiring a national identity through history lessons). In other words, schools are responsible for transmitting a '**collective conscience**' to young individuals.

Parsons extends this analysis further by arguing that:

- schools act as a 'bridge' between familial roles and social roles;
- schools allocate roles – they grade people according to ability.

It is widely agreed that the family is responsible for the **primary socialisation** of children, who learn the values of that family. However, the school develops and transmits society's values, which are **universal** (applicable to all), where status is earned rather than just given. Children have to learn to co-operate with people outside the family. School prepares young people for this transition by offering individuals the chance to compete on a 'level playing field', regardless of ascribed characteristics, to acquire knowledge and skills which can be utilised in wider society. Furthermore, the acquisition of qualifications encourages and rewards achievement – the giving of different rewards for different levels of achievement mirrors the way in which society operates.

Schools, therefore, act as a 'matchmaker' for talents and occupations. **Primary schools** assume responsibility for sorting children according to general level of ability, whereas **secondary schools** establish more specific skills and suitability for adult careers.

However, it is on this final point that the functionalist **Hargreaves** finds an inherent contradiction. If schools fail to fulfil the '**cohesive**' function as described by **Durkheim**, they can be described as dysfunctional. Hargreaves argues that schools do not foster the communal and co-operative spirit that Durkheim advocates. Instead, individuals are encouraged to compete with one another. Essentially, this is a hostile and divisive practice, especially for those students who fail, drop out (through absenteeism) and enter into a pattern of **deviance** (which is also dysfunctional). Labour's education minister, David Blunkett, who proposed a number of measures to curb truancy for the very reasons highlighted above, also shares Hargreaves' concerns.

 In contrast to the functionalist position, the **Marxists Bowles and Gintis** argue that:

- education is not meritocratic but dependent on social class;
- education is a restricting rather than liberating process, which reproduces labour power (for the benefit of the ruling class).

Bowles and Gintis' first criticism of the education system is that educational attainment is (wrongly) assumed to be based on an individual's intelligence quotient (IQ – the ability to reason and problem-solve). They argue that IQ accounts for only a small part of educational attainment and that people with similar IQs but different class backgrounds do not achieve the same levels of success. Those who occupy a higher class position (with better financial resources) are more likely to stay in education longer, gain further and higher qualifications and develop their IQ as a consequence. Therefore, the notion that educational and occupational success is based on individual merit (or personal failure) is a myth – education reproduces and justifies inequality and privilege.

They also argue that education is subservient to the needs of the ruling class (described as the '**correspondence principle**'). Education is organised in such a way that it produces obedient, hard-working and highly motivated workers. They describe this as the '**hidden curriculum**' because rather than offering opportunities of self-development it conditions people for the workplace. For example, school, like work, is not a pleasurable experience for most people. So pupils learn to be motivated by external and instrumental rewards (i.e. qualifications and certificates) rather than fulfillment.

As **Marx** argued, work in capitalist society is an alienating (and thus unsatisfying) experience and workers are encouraged to take satisfaction from elsewhere (leisure pursuits). In addition, the separation and compartmentalisation of subjects in schools reflects the division of knowledge and skills in the workplace. Pupils, like workers, are not encouraged to take a holistic approach to life but accept the organising principle of society. As a consequence, a fragmented workforce are denied knowledge of the overall process and technically (and intellectually) unable to challenge or overthrow those who own and control the means of production. Finally, it is worth acknowledging that for Marxists, school itself is not the problem. They propose fundamental changes to the organisation and structure of the economy – it is capitalism that is the problem.

In *Learning to Labour*, **Willis**, working from a Marxist paradigm but using an interactionist methodology, argues that:

- education is not a particularly successful agency of socialisation;
- it has unintended consequences.

In contrast to the above **structural** accounts of education, Willis shows in his study that the pupils whom he refers to as 'lads' are neither completely subservient and docile nor empty vessels. Instead, they are active in defining their own responses to the educational system, which often fails to constrain them. They resist and create a **counter-school culture**, which is diametrically opposed to the values of the school. This is characterised by 'bunking off', doing as little work as possible and generally 'having a laugh'.

It would seem that on one hand that the education system is failing to mould 'ideal' workers, but on the other, the lads' rejection of school makes them suitable for manual work. In other words, their response to school reproduces the sort of labour required, but not directly or intentionally. Their behaviour in school not only acts as a coping mechanism to deal with the monotony of school life but it reflects and assimilates them into the **shop-floor culture**. Willis contends that the lads see through the veil of meritocracy, knowing that hard work at school will not be converted into considerable occupational or economic gains. Instead they choose to see out their time at school and enter the masculine world of manual work as soon as possible. In conclusion, Willis argues that through their own resistance the lads actually entrap themselves by contributing to their own exploitation and subordination.

 The **liberal** perspective proposes that education should:

- encourage individuals to develop their full potential;
- reduce inequality.

One major criticism of the education system is that pupils do not develop their critical faculties – instead teachers impose knowledge on them. The political and social supposition behind such ideas is that **progressive** education is vital for a successful democracy because people need to learn to think for themselves (for example, when voting). Education should also reduce inequality by developing educational programmes for the underprivileged and the poor.

The radical liberal **Illich**, in *Deschooling Society*, argues that formal schooling is both unnecessary and harmful to society because:

- it is irrelevant
- it indoctrinates individuals so that they become passive consumers.

Illich argues that schools should do two things that they do not do at present. First, they should 'teach' specific skills that reflect people's surroundings and needs. Illich regards most academic qualifications as irrelevant because they do not actually 'prove' professional competence (but manipulation). Second, education should be a liberating experience, whereby individuals can use and develop their own initiative. Instead, schools stifle creativity and imagination.

Illich's work, echoing the work of some **Marxist** thinkers, contends that schools, or more specifically the 'hidden curriculum', imposes values on students that serve the needs of consumer capitalism. The process of education – passivity in the classroom and the encouragement of a work effort towards external rewards – means that consumerism becomes an end in itself; education creates consumers rather than citizens.

He proposes a drastic overhaul of the system. Schools should be abandoned and replaced by '**skill exchanges**', where everyday 'life' skills are taught by '**experts**' from the local community rather than teachers. Furthermore, to encourage creative thinking, students working in groups should dictate activities and problem-solving.

4 The **social democratic** perspective on education has the following features:

- it has influenced educational reforms in Britain (particularly up to the mid-1970s)
- it holds that freedom of opportunity does not exist – **state** intervention is necessary

The social democratic position, derived from liberalism, is largely prescriptive. As we shall see in a later sections, there is a strong correlation between class position and educational success. The aim has been to minimalise these inequalities in opportunities and rewards by encouraging young people to develop and realise their full potential. The central tenet of this perspective is that social mobility can be achieved by benefiting individuals, as can a greater commitment and contribution to the prosperity of society. It was on this premise that the socially divisive tripartite system, with the choice of school for a child being based on the 11+ exam, was phased out and replaced by secondary comprehensives (i.e. the same schooling for all).

5 The **interactionist** perspective is concerned with:

- the day-to-day interaction of pupils and teachers;
- the process of labelling.

In contrast to structural interpretations, which imply that people are influenced by factors over which they have little control, the interactionist position focuses on what actually goes on in the classroom. A number of studies (for example **Rosenthal**) have concentrated on the **self-fulfilling prophecy**, showing how teachers' expectations and resultant interaction with pupils may determine how well the pupils will do. If pupils are labelled as hard-working conformists, not only are they likely to benefit from preferential treatment, but their concept of self will alter as well. Positively labelled pupils are likely to embrace their status, whereas negatively labelled pupils grudgingly accept theirs. The 'deviant' pupil is treated accordingly and may be deprived of knowledge as a consequence (which reaffirms the 'deviant' or lowly status).

This model suggests an absence of the pupil in negotiating roles; in other words it appears to be a one-way process initiated by those who have the power to label. For example, research has raised a number of questions about the validity of equal opportunities in education. It has been shown that there is a middle-class bias to the labelling process, which explains why middle-class students, who are seen as 'natural' student material, do better than their working-class counterparts (**Cicourel**). However, **Woods**' study focuses on how students adopt or negotiate certain roles within the school, which suggests a degree of self-determination. Similarly, **Fuller**'s work shows how black female students resent and challenge stereotypical labels by working hard and achieving academic success.

Class and differential achievement is primarily concerned with:

- explaining why some groups of people do better than others;
- examining how class can act as a barrier to educational achievement.

A central theme of the sociology of education is the attempt to explain why research study after research study has shown that the higher social class somebody belongs to the higher the levels of educational achievement. As **Halsey, Heath and Ridge**'s comprehensive study showed, the sons of professional fathers were ten times more likely to attend university than the working class son. To some degree, the functionalist account assumes that **meritocracy** exists and is reflected in a pupil's natural ability and genetic inheritance (which also accounts for their parents' class position). However, many sociologists, especially those working within a **Marxist** paradigm, treat this with a degree of scepticism. For example, **Bowles and Gintis**' contention is that class rather than IQ is the most important factor in determining how successful a student will be. Moreover, IQ testing is a social construction; it has an inbuilt bias against those who have a different cultural background from those who constructed it.

If we immediately dismiss IQ, how else can we explain the differences in educational attainment? **Bourdieu** argues that:

- middle and upper class students have a distinct advantage – **cultural capital**;
- working class failure is the fault of the education system.

Bourdieu's main assertion is that schools are middle-class institutions run by middle-class people in which middle-class pupils succeed. The **dominant culture** (knowledge that has been defined as worthy and superior), with which the middle classes have an affinity, forms the basis of the education system, and so students from these social groups have a distinct advantage.

Working-class students do not share the same **habitus** (way of living) as the middle-class students. In other words, they do not acquire or possess cultural capital – knowledge that can be translated into educational success and later into power and wealth. As a consequence, working-class culture is seen as an aberration and devalued by schools. Their lack of **cultural capital** (knowledge of dominant culture) disadvantages them immediately and continues to act a barrier to learning, which means they are more likely to fail exams. By failing what appear to be 'fair' exams, people voluntarily opt out of a system which is unlikely to benefit them. After all, is it worth continuing in education and deferring earning money today if in five years time you are in no better a position? Furthermore, working-class failure is contrasted with the educational success of the middle classes and it is upon this basis that privilege can be justified and legitimised.

7 In **Bernstein**'s analysis of speech patterns he suggests that:

- there are two forms of speech patterns: elaborated code and restricted code;
- working class children are limited to restricted code.

Like Bourdieu, Bernstein argues that middle-class students have a distinct advantage over working-class students because school is conducted through an **elaborated code** (language that is precise, elaborate and detailed). The crux of Bernstein's analysis is that middle-class people are more likely to use the elaborated code, so children with this background are conversant with it already – they are well practised before they enter the school gates. On the other hand, working-class children use more informal language, known as the **restricted code**. It is deemed unsuitable in school and immediately disadvantages them from acquiring the skills demanded by the education system (and impedes further progress).

A number of studies have shown that the middle-class home offers a better **environment** for educational success. Obviously, those from financially better-off homes benefit from enjoying better resources, for example access to books, computers (and so the Internet) and appropriate places to study. Moreover, the parents' experience of and attitudes towards education are likely to be defining factors too. Middle-class parents, who are more likely to have benefited from the educational system, are more likely to show an interest, encourage and help their children. It is not suggested that working-class parents do not care or will not make provisions, but in many cases they cannot offer the same financial and (possibly) intellectual assistance as their middle-class counterparts. In addition, **Sugarman** argues that working-class culture emphasises instant gratification rather than deferment and planning, which affects attitudes towards education and careers.

Patterns related to gender in educational achievement can also be identified and attributed to how **males** and **females** are socialised in schools. Research has found that the gender divisions of socialisation are perpetuated in the classroom; from the way students are treated because of their sex to the dominance of 'sexist' literature that positions men and women in 'traditional' roles. According to **Spender**, men's knowledge and experiences are seen as superior in the sexist curriculum. Furthermore, it has been found that teachers hold a stereotypical view of the male 'breadwinner' and female 'homemaker', which dictates the nature of the interaction. As a consequence, girls tend to underestimate their ability and receive less attention from teachers.

However, statistics show (*Social Trends 28,* 1995/96) that on average girls leave school with a higher number of GCSEs (10% more) and A Levels (3% more) than boys. This suggests there has been a shift in attitude towards female social roles. For instance, there is a wider understanding of what constitutes **sexual discrimination** by teachers and pupils alike, which may have led to changes in teaching practices. In addition, de-industrialisation has brought about changes in the job market. This has resulted in an increase in career opportunities for females and acted as an incentive to gain qualifications. These changes are reflected in changing attitudes amongst women. They are more likely to expect to become independent, have a job or career and support themselves rather than relying on the traditional higher paid male breadwinner.

Sociological work into **ethnic minority educational attainment** is concerned with explaining:

* how cultural background can act as a barrier;
* how prejudice and discrimination limit educational opportunities.

The Swann Report showed that whilst Asian children in Britain do almost as well as white children, West Indian children do considerably worse (only 5% passed an A Level and only 1% went to university). As we have seen, most sociologists attribute educational success to environmental and cultural factors (many ethnic minority people are also working class). For instance, many Asian families and parents are seen as having high aspirations and being more supportive of their children's efforts in education. On the other hand, **Pryce** describes West Indian families as 'turbulent' and less close-knit.

Within the classroom, other problems can be encountered. The Swann Report found that some (predominantly white) teachers were unintentionally racist by holding common stereotypical views of ethnic minority students. In other words, they expected them to have disciplinary problems (**Brittan**) and do badly. This '**institutional racism**' is exacerbated by the language conventions (or speech patterns) used by schools (see Bernstein above). **Coard** argues that West Indian children are taught that black culture and ways of speaking are inferior to 'normal' school discourse. Moreover, if English is not the household's dominant language this problem becomes more acute and holds children back still more. By showing an inflexible attitude to language, schools are effectively ostracising certain groups, who may as a consequence develop a sense of inferiority because they appear to lack the qualities that are required for academic success.

9 Over the last 20 years, education has become an important political issue in Britain. Critics of the education system have accused it of 'failing' – the system either fails the individual or it fails the nation, or more specifically the economy. The most important single influence on education in this period was the implementation of 'new right' policies, known as **new vocationalism**, which were less concerned with providing equal opportunities and more concerned with linking education to the economy. The aim was to create a 'market mentality' so that schools became more competitive and provided increased choice (especially parental choice). The supposition behind the introduction of market forces was that schools would compete for (typically, the best) students. This was accompanied by the introduction of a **national curriculum** and standardised tests, the results of which are published in **league tables** to enable consumers (parents and students) to make an informed choice.

Critics of these reforms have argued that league tables discriminate against those schools whose catchment area is predominantly made up of disadvantaged groups. For 'poorer' schools (academically and financially) the publication of league tables can affect the morale and self-esteem of the whole school. As a consequence, there is a risk that brighter students may leave, which may further exacerbate the school's problems.

Furthermore, the concept of choice is one that is constrained by the introduction of the national curriculum – students in state schools have to follow it, whereas those in private institutions do not. Choice, it would seem, is only available to the more affluent members of society. Those who attend private schools and colleges often have considerable advantage over those who attend state-run institutions, enjoying better facilities, smaller classes and more individual attention. Moreover, high status public schools (such as Eton, Harrow or Winchester) not only provide superior educational opportunities but also contacts with those who belong to the higher echelons of society.

30 minutes

 your knowledge

 1 Compare and contrast the Marxist and functionalist accounts of education.

 2 Why are middle-class children more likely to succeed at school than working-class children?

 3 How did education change in the 1980s and 1990s?

Theories and Methods

Broadly, there are two ways of conducting sociological research. Quantitative research provides numerical data, whereas qualitative methods offer detail and insight. The problems that sociology has to contend with is that society is its laboratory and people its specimens. There are many ethical reasons why sociologists cannot put humans into a laboratory and it is this that limits sociology's claim to being a science.

 Identify two other reasons why sociologists cannot observe human behaviour in laboratory conditions. (2 marks)

 What are the advantages and disadvantages of quantitative and qualitative approaches to sociology? (9 marks)

 Is sociology a science? (9 marks)

Socialisation, Identity and Youth and Culture

Some scholars argue that gender differences are natural and inevitable. It is the contention of the thinkers Tiger and Fox that men and women are genetically pre-programmed to behave the way they do. Men inherit genes that make them the 'hunter', whereas women are naturally 'caring', 'motherly' and 'homemakers'. This justifies the differences for men and women's roles in modern society.

 In general, which sociological theory echoes the above statement? (5 marks)

Are social roles natural and inevitable? (15 marks)

Sociology of The Family and Households

It is commonly argued by some sociologists that the nuclear family is universal because its arrangement is beneficial to the whole of society. It acts as an emotional release or a haven in a heartless world, where people can escape from the tensions of work and the pressures of everyday living. However, this tension is often carried into the home. Sometimes the man directs his frustrations at his wife or partner. This 'expression' or 'release' is just one example of 'patriarchal power'.

Which two sociological perspectives would you associate with the statement above? (4 marks)

 What do we mean by the 'dark side' of family life? (8 marks)

Is the modern family symmetrical? (8 marks)

Sociology of Religion

Religion is no longer the 'opiate of the masses'. Religion is dead. It no longer has the hold on society that it once did. No longer do we bow in deference to our religious leaders. Instead we turn to pop stars for inspiration. Politicians only refer to the church whenever they need to morally underpin their argument. The Church, like an old lapdog, will wander over to whoever calls it. It is no more than a weak and toothless pressure group.

 Which thesis is being described above? (1 mark)

 What evidence is there to suggest that religion is dead? Illustrate your answer with examples. (9 marks)

 According to structural accounts, religion is a conservative force. Do you agree? (10 marks)

Mass Media and Popular Culture

There is an ongoing debate about the effects of the mass media. The 'moral majority', represented by the National Viewers and Listeners Association, argues that the mass media undermines the norms and values of society. For example, *Child's Play 3* was implicated by the trial judge and newspapers as a contributory factor to the actions of the children who killed James Bulger. This is similar to another position which argues that the media acts in favour of the ruling classes by making people passive.

What model is being described above? (1 mark)

(i) Give examples of two studies which have found a link between media consumption and subsequent behaviour. (4 marks)

(ii) Why are these studies problematic? (4 marks)

 Do you agree that the audience is active rather than passive? (11 marks)

Health

Illness is more prevalent in some social groups than others, which suggests to sociologists that health is a social construction. Some right-wing thinkers argue that poor health is a consequence of people's conscious actions. They argue that people have choices and if they choose to eat fatty and nutritionally deficient foods and smoke and drink in large quantities then it is no wonder that they will suffer from bad health and illness. Illnesses related to poor diet, smoking and drinking are most commonly found in the working class, especially men.

 Which variations in health can be attributed to gender differences? (4 marks)

 How far would you agree with the statement that 'poor health is a consequence of people's conscious actions'? (10 marks)

How useful is the interactionist approach to the study of the sociology of health? (6 marks)

Work

The nature of work has changed beyond recognition. 'Post-Fordist' workers are characterised as those that possess a 'portfolio of skills'. The key to business success is flexibility. Workers, like companies, should not only react to but also embrace the revolution in the workplace.

 What is 'post-Fordism'? (6 marks)

How do Marxist accounts of changing work practices contrast with the functionalist account? (6 marks)

 In recent years, the implementation of new work practices and structures has resulted in job losses and consequently industrial action. Referring to sociological thought, can industrial action be justified? (8 marks)

Exam Practice Questions

Education

Numerous sociological studies have shown that class position can be correlated with educational attainment. Bowles and Gintis showed that educational success is more dependent on class than IQ. Bourdieu attributes this to 'cultural capital' possessed by middle-class students. Schools are described as middle-class institutions, which fail working-class pupils.

1 Why is IQ testing problematic? (3 marks)

2 What is meant by the term 'cultural capital'? (5 marks)

3 Compare and contrast structural and interpretative accounts of the differential in educational achievement. (12 marks)

Answers on page 90

Use Your Knowledge Answers

The following suggestions are guides to the content of suitable and appropriate answers.

Theories and Methods

 Is sociology a science?

You should consider the following:

- how science is defined;
- how sociology has tried to emulate the methods of science;
- Popper's view that sociology cannot be a science because it does not try to disprove itself – it is too preoccupied with theory rather than conducting research;
- Kuhn's view that science operates in paradigms;
- the new realists who suggest that the sciences and sociology share an interest in 'open' systems.

It is worth remembering that many sociologists, particularly those with a social action perspective, are not preoccupied with achieving 'scientific' knowledge.

Account for the differences between structural and social action theories.

You should:

- Describe structural theories (namely, Marxism and functionalism) – how they offer 'macro' explanations (how institutions impact on individuals).
- Describe social action theories (derived from Weber) – how they concentrate on the interaction between individuals and the meanings they generate from these encounters.
- Mention that both have advantages and disadvantages: structural accounts are described as being too deterministic and over reaching; although 'micro' studies focus on the complex nature of the interaction between individuals, they are often described as not representative enough.

Use Your Knowledge Answers

Socialisation, Identity and Youth Culture

1 *Are social roles natural and inevitable?*

You should consider:

- the social biology argument (Tiger and Fox) – behaviour is genetically inherited and evolutionary, which explains the differences between men and women (this is close to the functional account, which justifies the division of labour);
- that socialisation is an inevitable process in which people learn the 'rules' of life – identities are social constructs;
- Marxist and feminist perspectives on how people acquire their social roles (it is also worth considering the role of class and ethnicity).

2 *Compare and contrast structural and interactionist theories of socialisation.*

You should consider:

- Marxist accounts – how people are socialised into the dominant culture;
- functionalist accounts – how people learn the norms and values of society;
- symbolic interactionism and ethnomethodology – how roles are negotiated between people.

3 *How is national identity constructed?*

You should consider:

- ideology – (Weiner) cultural inventions;
- education – history lessons;
- the media – portrayals of sports events.

4 *Youth culture no longer displays resistance. Discuss.*

You should consider:

- adolescence – transition from childhood to adulthood;
- earlier sub-cultural studies and patterns of resistance;
- Willis' and McRobbie's ideas on post-modern youth identities.

Sociology of the Family and Households

1 *The nuclear family is universal. Discuss.*

- Murdock argues that the family is universal. Functionalist analysis argues that as the most basic institution it is the most effective (describe how it works). It exists in many cultures/countries – persuasive argument.
- Consider cultural and deliberate exceptions – the Nayar, 'Russian Experiment' and kibbutzim.
- Consider the increasing number of single-parent families and the impact of divorce.
- Mention that no alternatives have lasted or replaced the concept of the family, particularly the mother-child bond.

2 *How has the composition of families changed over the last three centuries?*

- Discuss the lack of consensus.
- Pre-industrial families tended to be extended – organised as a unit of labour, status is ascribed. However evidence suggests that not all families were like this (Laslett).
- Early industrial families became smaller and kinship and neighbourhood ties were gradually eroded due to migration.
- Parsons describes the isolated modern family as necessary for the demands of modern industrial society. If the family remained structured on old principles of size and status, it would cause huge friction.
- Harris contends that the nuclear family provided the ideal basis for industrialisation, rather than being created as a result of industrialisation.

3 *Is the family the best organisational basis for society?*

- Functionalists promote the family as having positive benefits for society (it acts as a haven, it is responsible for socialisation).
- Marxists argue that the family is exploitative (Marx and Engels).
- Feminists concentrate on the 'double exploitation' of women. They also focus on the 'dark side' of family life – abuse (physical and mental) – women gain very little from it.
- Social psychologists (Leach and Laing) describe the family's negative effect on sociology – i.e. teaching simple but dangerous distinctions ('ghetto'). Relationships in the family are also likened to a 'Mafiosi' situation.

Sociology of Religion

1 *Is religion a necessary conservative force?*

- The functionalist account stresses the cohesive qualities of religion.
- The Marxist account describes religion as sustaining the status quo.
- Weber's work stresses that religion can act as a 'motor' of change. There are other examples where religion has helped to reform the social order (the Catholic church in Poland, Archbishop Tutu in South Africa).

2 *Assess the arguments for and against secularisation.*

- Wilson identifies the declining influence of church (socially and politically) – fewer people attending church and choosing religious ceremonies.
- Martin argues that secularisation is a dated argument – it is hard to prove.
- The introduction of religions (for example, Islam) into Britain has revitalised the debate.

3 *How can the organisation of a religion affect its life span?*

- Churches have longer life spans.
- Sects and cults that rely on a charismatic leader will break up when he or she dies.
- Millenarian movements (those waiting for Armageddon) have an inbuilt short life span.

Mass Media and Popular Culture

 1 **'It's not what the media does to people, it's what people do with the media that counts.' How true is this statement?**

- Describe and raise questions about 'effects' research – i.e. problematic methodology.

- Too general, elitist (Frankfurt School); some people have a moral agenda

- Think about the change in approach – Katz and Lazersfeld, McQuail, Blumer and Brown and Morley – decoding relies on the social characteristics of the audience, who will offer preferred, negotiated and oppositional readings.

 2 **Is ownership and control of the media important?**

There are two sides to the debate:

- The instrumental model contends that ownership counts, it influences content – cite evidence (e.g. Rupert Murdoch) – too much power in the hands of few people threatens democracy.

- The structural/determination approach contends that it is the economy that dictates the content of media output. Also, it is run by managers not owners. The pluralist account argues that the media responds to audiences' demands. The rich variety of media forms and texts reflects this.

 3 **Discuss the representations in the media of two social groups.**

- Describe representations, discuss historical and ideological influences and give examples.

- Representations of women tend to place them in the traditional role of supporting men. Women are judged on the basis of appearance rather than ability.

- Ethnic minorities tend to be portrayed negatively – e.g. documentaries focus on racism, problems of immigration – or in stereotypical roles, e.g. sportsmen, musicians.

Health

 What sociological explanations are given for different levels of health and illness in different social groups?

- Link poverty with poor health (exacerbated by lack of money, poor housing, etc.)

- Discuss lifestyle choices: Bourdieu and 'habitus'.

- Mention right-wing critics' belief that poor health is a matter of choice.

- Look at different patterns in male/female smoking and drinking.

 Compare and contrast the functionalist and Marxist accounts of healthcare provision.

- Functionalism sees illness as dysfunctional. Health is best served by the monopoly of health professions to get people back to fulfilling their social roles.

- Marxism sees healthcare as a 'tool' of the ruling class. It is also a commodity to be bought and sold. Monopolies control the health market and exploit a 'need'.

 Evaluate the interactionist contribution to the sociology of health.

It shows how negotiation between doctors and patents can determine the outcome of health care.

Work

Describe and account for the changes in work practices over the last 30 years.

- Describe the shift from Fordism to post-Fordism.

- Define Fordism: production lines, large-scale inflexible working conditions, hierarchies.

- Define post-Fordism: flatter hierarchies, newer technologies, flexibility and diversity in working practices.

- Describe the negative effects: de-skilling, more control of workers, lack of certainty.

How do functionalist and Marxist accounts of work differ?

- Marxist: work is exploitative, profit is earned from surplus value of labour, alienation because workers have no control over what they produce.

- Functionalist: consensus relies on the interdependence and co-operation of workers – most people accept work for the greater good of society.

Why did unemployment increase in the 1980s?

- Mention disagreement about the rate of unemployment.

- Discuss changes in economic base – de-industrialisation, new technology, etc.

- Discuss changes in government economic policies (Keynesian to monetarist policies).

Education

 Compare and contrast the functionalist and Marxist accounts of education.

- Functionalism: education responds to the needs of society; it socialises people and sorts them for later occupations; it stresses the need for co-operation.

- Marxist thinkers, particularly Bowles and Gintis, describe the 'hidden curriculum', where working class people are trained to be docile, obedient workers. Educational success is not based on intelligence but on class.

 Why are middle-class children more likely to succeed at school than working-class children?

- The middle classes enjoy a number of advantages. Mention Bourdieu (cultural capital) and Bernstein (speech codes). Also, middle-class parents invest more time and effort and can provide better resources for children (places to study, books, computers).

- Working-class culture places less emphasis on education.

 How did education change in the 1980s and 1990s?

- The social democratic model 'failed'. It was replaced by 'new vocationalism' – linking education with work.

- Also, a competitive ethic was introduced to education. Schools had to compete for students. League tables of academic performance were published to facilitate 'customer' choice.

Theories and Methods

1 Humans will not behave naturally. It is an artificial environment.

2 Quantitative research can be large-scale, is usually quick to administer, produces numerical data upon which long-term trends can be found and could be said to be as objective as possible. However, the data can be limited and still relies on interpretation. People may lie or feel that they cannot express themselves. Qualitative research is based on the small-scale (micro) offering a thick description/insight to life, which surveys cannot. However, it is deemed to be unscientific because there is a real danger that the researcher can become too close to the subjects. Also, it can be deemed to be unethical if the researcher adopts a covert approach. Overt non-participation may have a detrimental effect on those being observed (Hawthorne effect).

3 Depends on definition. Answers should look at the methods open to the natural sciences and sociology. The discussion should include Popper's rebuke. Kuhn's work on paradigms should be cited, as should the new realists.

Socialisation, Identity and and Youth Culture

1 Answer should refer to functionalism, particularly Murdock, who argues that sex role-allocation (division of labour) is the most natural, thus best, organising principle on which families are based. The family passes on these roles from one generation to another for the maintenance and good of society.

2 Answers should acknowledge the natural physical/chemical differences between men and women. However, answers should refer to sociologists who argue that any role is a social construction (especially gender roles). Answers should also focus on class, national and ethnic identities by referring to commonly held stereotypes.

Sociology of The Family and Households

1 Functionalism and feminism.

2 The 'dark side' of family life is one which is focused on by feminists and the social psychologists Leach and Laing. Whilst feminists focus on the abuse (mental and physical) hidden by the 'ideology of the family', Leach and Laing focus on the damaging psychological effects it has on the members. Also, it is argued that in many cases the family is a divisive rather than socially unifying institution.

Exam Practice Answers

 Answers should focus on the development of the family, and how roles have appeared to change. Central to the debate is Willmott and Young's assertion that the family is symmetrical (i.e. roles are shared). In riposte, Marxist and feminist accounts argue that the family is still an exploitative arrangement for women.

Sociology of Religion

 The secularisation thesis.

 Less attendance at formal religious institutions; people are less likely to choose religious venues for marriages and less likely to have children baptised. The church is less powerful – it has little or no influence on government. However, this can be counteracted by the growth of 'new' religions in Great Britain, which are central to many people's lives. Also it is hard to judge if people are less religious.

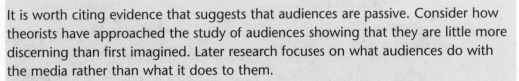 Marxists argue that religion justifies the present order and thus props up capitalism. The functionalist account argues that it helps maintain social equilibrium by acting as an emotional 'blanket' in potentially turbulent moments. In contrast, Weber argued that religion could actually act as a 'motor' of change.

Mass Media and Popular Culture

Hypodermic needle effect.

(i) Bandura (bobo doll) and Belson (diaries).

(ii) Bandura's study is problematic because it was set in laboratory and the children may have acted to please the researcher. Belson's study relied on the memories of films watched and linked with the boys' accounts of violent behaviour. Were the boys telling stories?

It is worth citing evidence that suggests that audiences are passive. Consider how theorists have approached the study of audiences showing that they are little more discerning than first imagined. Later research focuses on what audiences do with the media rather than what it does to them.

Health

 Answers should concentrate firstly on biological differences and related illnesses (e.g. testicular cancer). Secondly, differences can be accounted for by different drinking, eating and smoking habits. Students may also want to refer to the 'male disease' of avoiding the doctor.

Answers should recognise that in some cases 'free choice' is a romantic idea. Students should refer to the limits that class and economic position could impose on individuals. Good answers should refer to Bourdieu, 'habitus' and his notion of trajectory.

 The interactionist approach to sociology offers an insight into how roles are negotiated between doctor and patient (related to class position) and how that may determine treatment. Studies by Rosenthal and Goffman look at how labelling mental health determines future engagement with the individual.

Work

 'Post-Fordism' describes the changes in work practices from standardised, inflexible, hierarchical work practices to more flexible conditions. It demands more flexible workers and short, instantly changeable production runs.

 A simple functionalist account would argue that the workplace has to adapt to technological change and demand. Marxists focus on the de-skilling of labour and increased alienation in the workplace. Answers should also mention the uncertainty of short-term working conditions.

 In times when redundancy is a continual threat, strikes are often in protest against planned redundancies. Strikes can be described as dysfunctional to society because they break the 'social contract' that binds people together with the same interests. For Marxists they are a welcome expression of working class solidarity. Dahl argues that strikes and union action are justifiable because they are a formalised, institutionalised form of conflict, which acts as a peaceful and progressive solution to disputes.

Education

 Often IQ tests are ethnocentric – they disadvantage groups of people who are not members of the dominant group. They also have a class bias.

 'Cultural capital' is knowledge which is convertible into economic capital/wealth. It is possessed by the middle classes whose values are much closer to the dominant class.

Structural accounts, namely functionalism and Marxism, focus on the impact that schooling has on individuals. Whereas functionalism enthuses about the school's roles in nurturing and developing social creatures, Marxists concentrate on its more insidious impact, turning individuals into conforming, unquestioning 'cogs' in the capitalist machine.

Notes

Notes